P9-CFF-012

Fourth Edition

A Study Guide to Epidemiology and Biostatistics

Richard F. Morton, MD, MPH
Formerly, Vice President for Medical Services
March of Dimes—Birth Defects Foundation
White Plains, New York

J. Richard Hebel, PhD
Professor
Department of Epidemiology and Preventive Medicine
University of Maryland School of Medicine
Baltimore, Maryland

Robert J. McCarter, ScD
Assistant Professor
Department of Epidemiology and Preventive Medicine
University of Maryland School of Medicine
Baltimore, Maryland

AN ASPEN PUBLICATION®
Aspen Publishers, Inc.
Gaithersburg, Maryland
1996

Library of Congress Cataloging-in-Publication Data

Morton, Richard F., 1924–
A study guide to epidemiology and biostatistics: includes 125
multiple-choice review questions / Richard F. Morton, J. Richard
Hebel, Robert J. McCarter.—4th ed.
p.   cm.
Includes bibliographical references and index.
ISBN 0-8342-0740-0
1. Epidemiology—Problems, exercises, etc.   2. Medical statistics—
Problems, exercises, etc.   I. Hebel, J. Richard (John Richard),
1935–   . II. McCarter, Robert J.   III. Title.
[DNLM: 1. Epidemiology—problems.   2. Statistics—problems.
WA 18.2 M891s 1996]
RA652.7.M67   1996
614.4—dc20
DNLM/DLC
for Library of Congress
95-44089
CIP

Editorial Services: Ruth Bloom

Library of Congress Catalog Card Number: 95-44089
ISBN: 0-8342-0740-0

Printed in the United States of America

1   2   3   4   5

Table of Contents

Preface

The two disciplines epidemiology and biostatistics are receiving increasing recognition for their ubiquity in problem solving. In this book we provide coordinated instruction in these subjects. We cover this material at a level that would enable the student to understand and critically read the health sciences literature. The final chapter introduces a systematic procedure to aid the student in the evaluation of such articles.

This book is intended for students of the entire spectrum of the health sciences, including medicine, nursing, dentistry, pharmacy, public and community health, and allied health sciences. It is appropriate for a variety of educational formats including both traditional and problem-based learning approaches. The scope and level are appropriate for students in professional schools, universities, four-year colleges, community colleges, and, in fact, any setting where courses in health sciences are taught. Our text is based on a course given to second-year students at the University of Maryland School of Medicine. Our students have found this book an effective study guide. It has been used successfully for individual, self-paced instruction by selected students.

Our book has a distinct method, based on pedagogic principles. The 45 objectives, expressed in behavioral terms, cite the concepts to be learned and the level at which students are expected to perform. There are three elements to the book, the first being the study notes. These notes may be read as the sole source of input to cover the material, or they may be used to supplement attendance at a lecture series. They are not designed to replace or compete with existing textbooks of epidemiology and biostatistics, which are specifically referenced following each chapter. (Students are encouraged to augment their learning by reference to these books.) The second element is the exercises that accompany each chapter. The exercises encourage students to immediately use their new-found knowledge, and this practice improves retention. Detailed feedback is provided in the exercise answers, which are amplified at points where we have learned that some students have difficulty. The third element in the instruction process is the multiple-choice examinations, which have the same scope and are on the same level that students may expect to encounter in professional examinations. Students are challenged both progressively as the material is covered and comprehensively in a final examination.

This edition now includes Chapter 17 on Keys to Understanding Articles on Epidemiologic Studies. It teaches the use of an overview constructed from the abstract as a guide for critical assessment of the paper. The procedure integrates and applies the principles introduced in the preceding chapters and provides a practical tool for the lifelong learner practicing evidence-based medicine.

Chapters 1 and 4 have been expanded to introduce the topic of "effect modification" (interaction). We provide detailed examples that will help the reader understand this sometimes difficult topic and differentiate it from another concept, confounding, with which it is traditionally confused.

In summary, we believe this new edition retains the clarity and succinctness of the previous editions while providing the reader with a reasonably comprehensive view of the mainstream concepts in epidemiology and biostatistics.

Acknowledgments

We thank the students of the University of Maryland School of Medicine for providing us with the experience necessary to make this book possible.

We also express our gratitude to Drs. Judith Rubin and Roger Sherwin for their suggested improvements to Chapter 17.

How To Use This Book

To the Student

We suggest that, as you begin each chapter, you first read the accompanying study notes. If they are not sufficiently detailed, please read the standard textbooks listed in the Recommended Readings for that chapter, which are cited in ascending order of difficulty.

Following each chapter are exercises; you should answer the questions, preferably writing down your responses, before consulting the solutions provided. When the first third of the book is completed, you will encounter a multiple-choice self-assessment exam consisting of 25 questions. Complete the exam and score your efforts (answers are given on page 199). You should score at least 60% before proceeding to the next chapters. If you should fail to achieve this level at your first attempt, we suggest that you restudy the sections with which you had difficulty. Similar self-assessment exams are provided following Chapters 11 and 17. A passing grade of 60% is also suggested for these. The final examination, covering all the objectives, may then be attempted. We suggest that 75% constitutes a passing grade on the total 125 questions and that 90% indicates an honor grade.

To the Instructor

This book is versatile. It may be used as a course textbook for a formal lecture series given to large groups. It also has a role in a seminar series, freeing the instructor from didactic teaching, thus enabling more complete discussion of relevant examples. It may be used as a vehicle for an independent study program in which the faculty member assumes the role of a tutor. The exclusive feature of our large question bank provides the instructor with a ready-made assessment instrument to monitor the progress of the students. Specific weaknesses may be identified and focal remediation given.

Goals and Objectives

Goals

After completing this study guide, the student will be able to

1. Apply epidemiologic methods to critically evaluate the evidence used in medical decision-making.
2. Assess data by using epidemiological and biostatistical principles and evaluate conclusions based on study data.

Objectives

1. Interpret the distribution of disease in a population according to time, place, and person.
2. Describe the composition of a rate, in terms of the numerator and denominator, and explain the relationship between them and the importance of time.
3. Explain the use of rates for comparative purposes.
4. Define *attack rate,* and use it to identify a vehicle of transmission in a common-source outbreak of disease.
5. Define *crude mortality rate, specific mortality rate* (age, sex, race, and cause), *case fatality rate,* and *proportionate mortality ratio.* Cite one example of the correct use of each of these rates, and interpret statements containing them.
6. Explain what is meant by confounding.
7. State the reasons for adjustment of rates, and interpret statements containing adjusted rates.
8. Define *incidence* and *prevalence;* state the relationship between them.
9. Name the factors that may cause variation in each measurement. Give the uses of each rate.
10. Define *absolute risk, relative risk,* and *attributable risk,* and interpret statements that employ these terms.
11. Explain what is meant by effect modification.

12. State the purpose of a frequency distribution and cumulative frequency distribution in describing a set of biological measurements.
13. Define *mean, median, mode,* and *percentile,* and describe the features of a distribution that each characterizes.
14. Contrast the features of a normal (Gaussian) distribution to those of a skewed distribution.
15. Explain why the mean ±2 standard deviations is often used to establish the "normal range" and what practical difficulties might be encountered using this procedure in clinical practice.
16. Determine probabilities from frequency distributions.
17. Explain what is meant by conditional probability.
18. Calculate the probability of complex events by applying the addition and multiplication rules.
19. Define *sensitivity, specificity,* and *predictive value* of a screening test, and compute these measures given the necessary data.
20. Describe the selection of screening test criteria with respect to the natural history of the disease in question.
21. Use the standard error to compute 95% confidence limits for a mean or a proportion, and interpret statements containing confidence limits.
22. Explain sampling bias, and describe how random sampling operates to avoid bias in the process of data collection.
23. Distinguish between the standard deviation and the standard error, and give one example of the use of each.
24. Interpret statements of statistical significance with regard to comparisons of means and frequencies, and explain what is meant by a statement such as "$P < 0.05$."
25. Distinguish between the statistical significance of a result and its importance in clinical application.
26. Interpret the relationship between two variables as displayed on a scattergram, distinguishing between positive, negative, and zero correlation.
27. Explain the information provided by a regression equation as well as that provided by a correlation coefficient.
28. Interpret statements of statistical significance with regard to the correlation coefficient.
29. Distinguish between a simple regression equation and a multiple regression equation.
30. Interpret the slope coefficients in a multiple regression as well as statements regarding their statistical significance.
31. Explain the information provided by the coefficient of determination.
32. Describe applications of the logistic and Cox proportional hazards regression models.
33. Distinguish between experimental and observational studies.

34. Describe a case-control (retrospective) study.
35. Describe cohort (prospective) and cross-sectional studies.
36. Define *cohort,* and recognize a cohort effect when interpreting cross-sectional data.
37. Describe a randomized clinical trial.
38. Describe the circumstances that require prospective studies to control for differences in time under observation.
39. Describe how the following methods control for differences in time under observation, and indicate what assumptions underlie each:
    a. Person-time
    b. Life table, Kaplan-Meier analysis
40. Describe the role of proportional hazards methods in survival analysis.
41. Illustrate with one example the concept of multifactorial causation of disease.
42. Define the following types of association:
    a. artifactual
    b. noncausal
    c. causal
43. Distinguish between association and causation, and list five criteria that support a causal inference.
44. Use the abstract of a journal article from the medical literature to create an overview that lists the study type, indicates the principal findings, and highlights the potential pitfalls.
45. Use the overview as a guide for the critical examination of the article.

1

Investigation of an Epidemic

Objectives Covered

1. Interpret the distribution of disease in a population according to time, place, and person.
2. Describe the composition of a rate, in terms of the numerator and denominator, and explain the relationship between them and the importance of time.
3. Explain the use of rates for comparative purposes.
4. Define *attack rate,* and use it to identify a vehicle of transmission in a common-source outbreak of disease.

Study Notes

Epidemiology is the study of the distribution and determinants of disease in human populations. We try to find out who gets the disease and why. For example, is the disease more frequent among men or women, young or old, rich or poor, blacks or whites? Did they get the disease because of a genetic trait, an occupational exposure, or a life-style habit, such as cigarette smoking?

Epidemiology differs from clinical medicine in two important regards: First, epidemiologists study groups of people, not individuals. Second, epidemiologists study well people, in addition to sick people, and try to find out the crucial difference between those stricken and those spared. What is the trait common to the sick, yet rare in the well? Epidemiologists weigh and balance, contrast and compare. To determine if a study is an epidemiologic study, you should look for a control or comparison group. To make a comparison, you need to develop a rate. A rate is time based and is computed as

$$\frac{\text{events in the specified time period}}{\text{population at risk in the specified time period}}$$

It is usually expressed as events per 1,000 individuals, or some other convenient base.

1

The numerator is merely the number of people to whom something happened (i.e., they got sick or died) in the population at risk. The numerator must be derived (i.e., be a subset) from the denominator. The denominator (the population at risk) has to be all the people at risk for the event. For mortality, the denominator is the entire population, because death is a universal risk, but in pregnancy rates, for example, the denominator would comprise only females in the reproductive age group.

Attack Rate

An attack rate measures the proportion of the population that develops disease among the total exposed to a specific risk over a specified time period:

$$\text{attack rate} = \frac{\text{number of people ill in the time period}}{\text{number of people at risk in the time period}}$$

In an outbreak of food poisoning, attack rates are computed for all items ingested. These attack rates are computed for those people who are exposed (i.e., ate the item studied) and, most importantly, those who are not exposed (i.e., did not eat the item studied), as shown in Table 1–1.

Table 1–1 Differential Attack Rates of Illness According to Food Histories in an Epidemic of Food Poisoning

Food	Persons Who Ate Specified Food			Persons Who Did Not Eat Specified Food			Difference in Attack Rates
	Number	Number Ill	Attack Rate (%)	Number	Number Ill	Attack Rate (%)	
Turkey	133	97	73	25	2	8	+65
Dressing	121	88	73	37	11	30	+43
Potatoes and gravy	127	92	72	31	7	22	+50
Peas	105	77	73	53	22	41	+32
Rolls	66	50	76	92	49	53	+23
Margarine	66	50	76	92	49	53	+23
Salads	4	1	25	154	98	64	−39
Desserts	36	22	61	122	77	63	−2
Sandwich	11	1	9	147	98	67	−58
Coffee	98	59	60	60	40	67	−7
Milk	18	12	67	140	87	62	+5

Source: Modified from Tong et al., 1962.

By inspecting attack rates for those who ate specific items, it is impossible to incriminate a single vehicle. Comparing the attack rates between those who ate and did not eat a specified food, however, is more informative. The last column on the right in Table 1–1 shows this difference. Simple differences in attack rates alone may not distinguish between causal and noncausal associations. For instance, both turkey and potatoes and gravy have large differences in their attack rates between those who ate and did not eat these foods.

To distinguish the separate effects of turkey and potatoes and gravy, it is necessary to cross classify, as is shown in Table 1–2. An examination of this table clearly incriminates turkey as the suspected vehicle because the difference in attack rates among those who ate and did not eat turkey is quite large whether they ate potatoes and gravy, whereas the reverse is not true.

Table 1–2 Attack Rates for Food Combinations

	Ate Turkey			Did Not Eat Turkey		
	Number	Number Ill	Attack Rate (%)	Number	Number Ill	Attack Rate (%)
Ate potatoes and gravy	127	92	72	0	0	—
Did not eat potatoes and gravy	6	5	83	25	2	8

Source: Modified from Tong et al., 1962.

The association between potatoes and gravy and food poisoning disappears when account is taken of turkey consumption.

Attack Rates

		Turkey	
		Yes	No
Potatoes and Gravy	Yes	High	Low
	No	High	Low

The food item potatoes and gravy was only implicated because of the strong tendency of people to consume that food item with turkey. An epidemiologist would say that turkey plays the role of a confounder. The concept of confounding, "guilt by association," is important and will be treated more fully in Chapter 2.

Suppose now that both the food items were mildly contaminated such that neither by itself would cause illness but taken together would. The subsequent attack rates are indicated below.

Attack Rates

Turkey

		Yes	No
Potatoes and Gravy	Yes	High	Low
	No	Low	Low

Here we observe that the effect of potatoes and gravy depends on the presence or absence of turkey. Likewise, the effect of turkey is dependent on potatoes and gravy. Epidemiologists refer to this sort of phenomenon as effect modification (see Chapter 4 for further discussion).

Investigation of an Epidemic

An epidemic occurs when there are significantly more cases of the same disease than past experience would have predicted for that place, at that time, among that population. Disease in the individual may be considered the outcome of the interaction of three factors: agent, host, and environment. A triad, time, place, and person, is also used in the investigation of disease in the community.

Cases of the disease may be classified according to these three categories:

1. time, which includes date of onset and duration of observation
2. place, which includes dwelling and workplace
3. personal characteristics, which include age, sex, and occupation

Scrutiny of the results of such classification enables one to recognize characteristics common among the sick and rare among the well.

Epidemic Curve

An epidemic curve gives a convenient picture of the epidemic, and certain limited deductions may be drawn. In a common-source outbreak, such as that just discussed, the time between the common exposure (e.g., the meal) and the peak of the cases approximates the incubation period of the disease. There are also few or no secondary cases, and the curve is unimodal (Figure 1–1).

However, in a typical infectious disease, such as measles, which is spread from person to person, the picture of propagation, as shown by an epidemic curve, is not as clear. In a closed community, such as a school, barracks, or ship, it may be possible to trace successive waves of propagation, each resulting in a new crop of cases, separated from the previous peak by an incubation period. The epidemic ceases when the supply of susceptibles is exhausted.

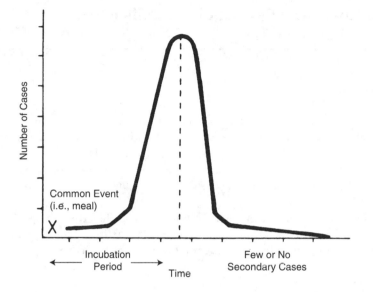

Figure 1–1 Common-Source Outbreak

Analysis

When the data have been collected, they may be analyzed as follows:

1. Plot an epidemic curve. Incubation periods may be estimated if times of exposure are known.
2. Calculate attack rates for different age, sex, and occupation categories.
3. Plot the geographic distribution of cases by residence and/or workplace.

On the basis of the analysis under 1, 2, and 3 above, a suspected vehicle may be identified. Attack rates may then be computed for those exposed and not exposed to this vehicle. However, sometimes this is not possible. For instance, in the investigation of a busy restaurant, the total exposed to a particular food is often unknown. In such instances, we compare, between the sick and a sample of the well, the proportions exposed to the suspected vehicle, as illustrated below.

At a restaurant, food poisoning occurred in 30 people, among whom 24, or 80%, ate raw oysters. This proportion alone is insufficient to incriminate oysters. It is necessary to investigate a sample of those diners not afflicted. Suppose we find that in 30 well diners, only 3, or 10%, ate the oysters. This comparison provides evidence consistent with the notion that eating oysters was the cause of the outbreak. Further study such as that outlined below would be necessary to substantiate that notion.

Exercises: An Outbreak of Jaundice in a Rural Community[1]

Introduction

On Friday, May 17, 1968, a request to assist in the investigation of an outbreak of infectious hepatitis was extended to the Hepatitis Unit of the Centers for Disease Control (CDC) in Atlanta, Georgia. It was learned that between April 30 and May 16, 1968, approximately 32 cases of infectious hepatitis had been reported to District #2 Health Department in North Trail, Michigan.

1. **Knowing that between April 30 and May 16, 1968, there were 32 cases of jaundice reported to the County Health Department, could you conclude that this is a problem of epidemic proportions? Why?**

Background

Lake County (Figure 1–2) is located in the northern portion of the lower peninsula of Michigan. The county has an area of 576 square miles and a population of 9,680 (1960 census), 2,025 of whom live in North Trail, the county seat. The area is predominantly rural, divided between farmland and forest.

The epidemic investigation was centered on the city of North Trail, in the southwestern portion of the county. There are only two other communities of notable size in Lake County: Spruce City, population 435, and Basco, population 308.

The remaining area is divided into 14 subdivisions, with the population being mostly in the low middle socioeconomic class; in the summer there is also a large tourist population.

Seven cases of infectious hepatitis were reported to the Michigan District #2 Health Department in the year prior to April 1968. Four of these cases occurred in one family outbreak in August 1967. The remaining three cases were scattered in time, and no relationship could be established between them.

2. a. **Are 32 cases in excess of normal expectancy?**
   b. **How do you establish whether this is greater than expected?**

---

[1]The information in this section was drawn from Schoenbaum, S. C., Baker, O., and Jezek, Z. 1976. Am. J. Epidemiol. 104:74. The place names have been changed.

Figure 1–2 Location of Lake County, Michigan

Epidemic Investigation

By May 19, there were 39 reported cases of hepatitis. By May 25 the number had risen to 61, and by June 1 the last two cases were reported, bringing the total to 63.

The first step in the investigation consisted of personally interviewing all reported hepatitis victims. All interviews were conducted by the same two investigators at the patients' homes. Patients were questioned about the date of onset of illness, symptoms of illness, previous exposure to cases of hepatitis, visits out of the community, and history of receiving injections of blood products. In addition, information was obtained for all other members of the family concerning recent illnesses and the administration of gamma globulin. The patients and their families were questioned about specific sources of water, milk, and food and about attendance at large gatherings or public places. At the time of the interview, a tap water sample was taken from each home for bacteriological analysis.

3. Ideally, what additional information should have been sought?

Epidemic Characteristics

Of Time

There were 63 cases of infectious hepatitis reported in Lake County between April 1 and May 8, 1968 (Figure 1–3). Of these, 61 had date of onset of illness between April 28 and May 26 (see Figure 1–3, which is an epidemic curve).

4. What inferences may be drawn regarding the probable time of initial exposure to the infection?

Of Person

The age- and sex-specific attack rates of Lake County cases with the date of onset of disease between April 28 and May 26 are illustrated in Table 1–3. Overall, the attack rate among males was almost twice as high as the attack rate among females, 8.1 per 1,000 versus 4.5 per 1,000 population, respectively.

Forty-three (70%) of the total Lake County cases occurred in schoolchildren, the remainder in the post-schoolchildren population. Thirty-six of the 43 school-

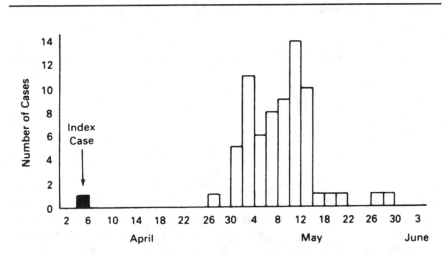

Figure 1–3 Cases of Infectious Hepatitis, April–May 1968, Lake County

Table 1–3 Attack Rates by Age and Sex in Cases of Infectious Hepatitis—Lake County, April 28–May 26

Age Group	Total Population by Age	Number of Cases			Attack Rate Per 1,000 Population		
		Male	*Female*	*Total*	*Male*	*Female*	*Total*
0–4	1740	0	0	0	0.0	0.0	0.0
5–9	1000	2	2	4	3.7	4.5	4.0
10–14	989	12	6	18	22.2	13.4	18.2
15–19	868	16	7	23	35.9	16.6	26.5
20–24	494	1	3	4	4.2	11.8	8.1
25–29	455	0	1	1	0.0	4.6	2.2
30–34	435	3	0	3	14.1	0.0	6.9
35–39	545	1	2	3	4.0	6.7	5.5
40–44	540	2	0	2	7.4	0.0	3.7
45–49	588	1	0	1	3.4	0.0	1.7
50–54	526	2	0	2	7.6	0.0	3.8
55+	1500	0	0	0	0.0	0.0	0.0
Totals	9680	40	21	61	8.1	4.5	6.3

children had attended the North Trail Public School. New cases occurred each at St. Luke's School, the Spruce City School, and the Basco School. There was one Lake County case at Brecken School in neighboring Penton County.

5. a. **How many cases were younger than 5 years old?**
   b. **Which decade of life had the highest attack rate?**
   c. **What hypothesis relative to time and person can you make at this point in this investigation?**

Of Place

Lake County has four school districts, two of which are extensions from adjacent Penton County. The largest district is the one served by the North Trail Public School (a single building complex located near downtown North Trail, serving 1,525 pupils in kindergarten through 12th grade). Seventy percent of the pupils of this school use the school buses. North Trail also has a Roman Catholic parochial school with 240 pupils, grades 1 through 8. This school uses the same buses as the North Trail Public School. Table 1–4 shows attack rates by grade for North Trail Public School and St. Luke's School. The attack rates are uniformly low through grade 6, but beginning in grade 7 there is an increase in the attack rates in the public school. The peak attack rate, 8.6%, occurred in grade 10, followed by substantially lower attack rates in grades 11 and 12. There is a marked difference in the attack rates between the 7th and 8th grade classes of the public and parochial school.

6. **What can you conclude from this information about the distribution of disease in terms of place?**

Analysis Related to Age

Note that Table 1–3 gives the frequency distribution of hepatitis cases by age and that Table 1–4 gives it by school and grade.

7. **Why is it important to calculate attack rates by age? Note once again that the majority of cases in Table 1–3 fall within the age group between 10 and 19 years, which is confirmed by the attack rates.**
8. **Using the information calculated about place and person, what conclusions can you draw now?**

Source of Epidemic

Using the information concerning time, place, and person, the investigators gathered relevant information concerning the school population. Children who

---

Table 1–4 Attack Rates by Grade and School in Cases of Infectious Hepatitis—Lake County, April 28–May 26

	North Trail Public School				Saint Luke's School		
Grade	Number in Class	Number Ill	Attack Rate (%)	Grade	Number in Class	Number Ill	Attack Rate (%)
K.	126	2	1.6				
1	128	0	0.0	1	37	1	2.7
2	121	0	0.0	2	41	1	2.4
3	107	0	0.0	3	37	0	0.0
4	106	2	1.9	4	26	0	0.0
5	120	1	0.8	5	30	0	0.0
6	111	1	0.9	6	32	0	0.0
7	110	3	2.7	7	26	0	0.0
8	120	6	5.0	8	21	0	0.0
9	143	7	4.9				
10	128	11	8.6				
11	112	1	0.9				
12	93	2	2.2				

attend kindergarten through grade 6 are not allowed to leave the campus for lunch. They may eat food prepared at the school cafeteria or may bring a lunch from home. Children in grades 7 through 12 at the North Trail High School, however, may leave the school during lunch hour. Since the school is only one block from the main street of North Trail, many students go downtown for lunch each day. St. Luke's School, however, does not allow any of its students, grades 1 through 8, to leave the campus for lunch. All parochial students must eat in the school cafeteria or bring lunch from home.

Convinced that there was a common source of exposure, the investigators began to look for a vehicle of transmission. The first major sources investigated were those of food and water. An exposure history is given in Table 1–5 of 41 hepatitis cases, aged 10 to 19, in Lake County in May 1968.

9. a. **From the information given in Table 1–5, what hypothesis can be formed about the source of the infection?**
   b. **Is this type of data alone sufficient to identify a single source?**

Food History of Well Individuals

To this point, the investigators concentrated on the sick individuals in the population. The attack rates were computed for specific food sources. To build a case, it is now necessary to examine food sources in the well population. By comparing the differential rates of exposure to sources between the well and the ill populations, an investigator should be able to further elucidate the true source of the infection.

10. a. **Examine Table 1–6. When the six listed exposures are compared, which source shows the largest differential between well and ill?**
    b. **Explain the high exposure rates to water in both the sick and well groups.**

Table 1–5 Exposure History of 41 Hepatitis Cases, Ages 10–19, Lake County, May, 1968

Food or Water	Yes	No	Unknown	Percent Known Exposed
Restaurant A	15	25	1	36.6
Restaurant B	17	23	1	41.5
North Trail Dairy Queen	28	12	1	68.3
Spruce City Dairy Queen	8	32	1	19.5
North Trail Bakery	37	3	1	90.2
North Trail municipal water supply	36	5	0	87.8

Table 1–6 Comparison of the Exposure History of 41 Cases of Hepatitis A in the 10- to 19-Year-Old Age Group with the Exposure History of a Group of 56 Well Household Members in the 10- to 19-Year-Old Age Group, Lake County, May 1968

	Hepatitis Cases			
	Number Yes	Number No	Number Unknown	Percent Known Exposure
Restaurant A	15	25	1	36.6
Restaurant B	17	23	1	41.5
North Trail Dairy Queen	28	12	1	68.3
Spruce City Dairy Queen	8	32	1	19.5
North Trail Bakery	37	3	1	90.2
North Trail water	30	5	0	87.8
	Well Household Members			
Restaurant A	22	31	3	39.3
Restaurant B	15	39	2	26.8
North Trail Dairy Queen	39	17	0	69.6
Spruce City Dairy Queen	6	50	0	10.7
North Trail Bakery	26	29	1	46.4
North Trail water	51	4	1	91.1

Milk Source

All commercial milk sold in Lake County comes from dairies located outside the county. None of the commercially produced milk in Michigan is limited to Lake County alone.

11. What conclusions can you draw about milk possibly being the source of the contamination?

Food Sources

Common exposure to a food item could explain the characteristics of this common-source outbreak. The only food items prepared and consumed locally are the foods served in the restaurants, salads sold in the delicatessens, Dairy Queen ice cream, and baked goods. Most of these products have been eaten at some time by the majority of the local residents. Almost all the cases who lived in Lake County gave a history of eating baked goods from the North Trail Bakery. However, it was impossible, from this information alone, to determine whether the bakery was the source of the epidemic or simply a very popular establishment in town.

12. Study Figure 1–4. How do these data aid in the investigation?

Review of Case Histories

To further study the problem, the investigators sought cases who lived outside Lake County. In any such investigation, detailed case histories often revealed supporting evidence.

Case 1 The subject was a 45-year-old female schoolteacher who lives in Purley, a town on Lake Huron, 60 miles from North Trail. Her only contacts with Lake County were when she passed through North Trail on March 20, April 5, and April 14 on the way to visit her father who lived on Lake Michigan's shore of the state. She stopped only on the first two occasions. On March 20, she had only a cup of coffee in a North Trail restaurant. On April 5, she bought some cupcakes and a coffee cake. On May 5 she became ill with hepatitis.

Case 2 A 35-year-old housewife who lives in Detroit, Michigan

Case 3 The eight-year-old daughter of Case 2

Case 4 A 49-year-old housewife who lives in Potomac is the sister-in-law of Case 2 and the aunt of Case 3. Both Case 2's family and Case 4's family own summer cottages in Lake County (10 to 15 miles from North Trail). They went to their cottages on April 8, 9, and 10 to open them for the season. At no time did Case 4 or Case 3 go in or near the city of North Trail. On April 9, Case 4 took care of Case 2's children while Case 2 went into the city to conduct some business. At that time Case 2 bought some pastries at the North Trail Bakery to bring to the cottage for lunch. All three cases ate the same kind of glazed donut. Case 2 and Case 3 became ill on May 7th, and Case 4 became ill on May 11. No other member of either family had the same kind of pastry, and no other member of either family is known to have been ill since being in Lake County.

Case 5 A 35-year-old mother of six purchased assorted glazed and iced products at the North Trail Bakery on April 6. She took the baked products home, where they were consumed by her and her family.

Cases 6 and 7 Case 5's two older daughters ate some of them.

Cases 8 and 9 Case 5's two youngest sons returned home later in the day and consumed all but one glazed item.

Case 10 Case 5's 5-year-old daughter and her twin came home and, after a dispute, Case 10 won possession of the glazed delicacy. She became ill, but her twin did not.

The father, who was away at work throughout the day, did not eat any of the bakery goods and remained well.

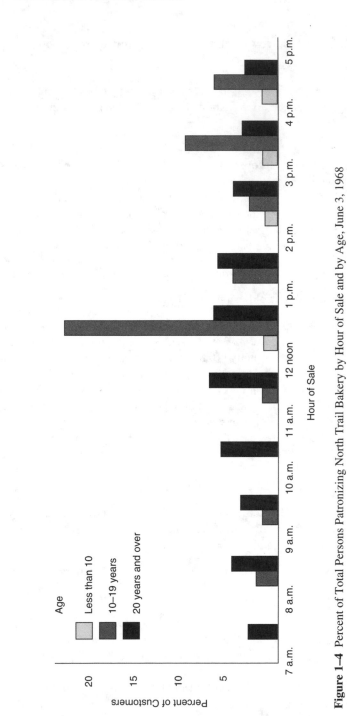

Figure 1–4 Percent of Total Persons Patronizing North Trail Bakery by Hour of Sale and by Age, June 3, 1968

13. Are the above data compatible with the bakery being the source of infection?

The occurrence of infectious hepatitis one month after direct exposure to the North Trail Bakery was illustrated by Case 1. Cases 3 and 4 showed that only contact with baked products could be associated with infectious hepatitis, because they had no contact with the North Trail municipal water supply, with any of the restaurants in North Trail, or with any other local food-handling establishment. None of these four cases had any history of contact with anyone known to have infectious hepatitis or jaundice. None had a history of infections or administration of blood products within six months prior to the onset of illness, and none had a history of recent ingestion of shellfish.

14. What would your next step in the investigation be?

One of the cases in Lake County was a baker's assistant. This 34-year-old white male is reported physically and mentally handicapped. He visited his physician on April 6, 1968, complaining of "vomiting and a cold." His wife visited the same physician two days later complaining of nausea and generalized headaches. The patient continued to work until April 11, when the diagnosis of infectious hepatitis was made. Co-workers at the bakery reported that the patient had dark urine for at least four days before he stopped working. He did not return to work until April 23. Figure 1–3 shows the complete epidemic. Note that the baker's assistant is the initial case (in black).

15. a. Does the epidemic curve reveal the incubation period for hepatitis?
    b. Does this curve still support a common source of infection?
16. Knowing that infectious hepatitis virus is killed by heat, what further investigation would you undertake to confirm the source of the virus?

Investigation of the Bakery

The North Trail Bakery has served the region for 34 years. It makes a variety of breads, pastries, donuts, cookies, pies, and cakes. Besides over-the-counter sales in downtown North Trail, the bakery supplies all sweet rolls and donuts and some of the bread to each of the restaurants in the North Trail area and to grocery stores in Lake County.

The baker's assistant helps in practically every process of the baked goods. In particular, he is responsible for making and glazing donuts and for icing much of the pastry. Observation by investigators revealed that icing was spread on the pastries by hand and items to be glazed were dipped into the glaze by hand. Since the pastry is not cooked further after glazing or icing, these processes are likely points of contamination.

Both glaze and icing may be kept for several days and old batches may be used to start new ones. Bakery products not sold in one day may be sold in the next business day as "day-old pastries" or may be frozen for sale in the next one to two weeks. Therefore, contaminated foods could be available for consumption over a period of several days or weeks. In the midst of the epidemic investigation, as it became clear that the bakery was an increasingly likely source, a blood sample was taken from each person who worked in the bakery to ascertain whether there were any cases of hepatitis present at the time in the bakery employees.

An SGPT (an enzyme test for liver function) was performed on each blood sample, and in all instances the SGPT was within normal limits. Because the epidemic curve showed that the outbreak was ending at this time (June 3) and because there was no elevated SGPT level found, the bakery was permitted to remain open.

17. **Do you agree with this decision? Support your view.**
18. **Since none of the bakery employees appeared ill, why were SGPT tests performed?**

Control Measures

Serum gamma globulin was immediately offered to all residents, and 7,000 to 8,000 doses were distributed after June 3, 1968.

19. a. **Since the epidemic had ended, why was it necessary to administer the gamma globulin?**
    b. **How would you evaluate the effectiveness of this control measure?**

Exercise Answers

1. **You cannot determine whether or not 32 cases of jaundice constitute an epidemic unless you know how many cases to expect in that place during that time.**
2. a. **Yes.**
   b. **That these cases are in excess of what may be expected, could be confirmed by a statistical test. However, usually the fact that four times the annual number of cases had occurred in a very short space of time is sufficient to warrant an investigation.**
3. **The additional information needed is similar data on a group of well individuals.**

4. We may assume that these cases were all exposed on or about the first week of April, about 30 days before peak.
5. a. No cases under 5 years old.
   b. 10- to 19-year olds had the highest attack rates.
   c. The attack rate is highest in males. The cases occur during a limited time period. The epidemic appears to be due to a common source to which children younger than school age were not exposed.
6. All but eight of the cases occurred in the North Trail school district. This suggests that the common experience of most cases may relate to attendance in North Trail schools.
7. Age as well as place may give clues to the mechanism of spread and the common experience that caused the outbreak. Age is also indicative of immune status from previous exposures.
8. The epidemic occurred primarily in North Trail School in the junior and senior high schoolchildren.
9. a. No inference can be drawn from Table 1–5, since there is neither a comparison group without disease nor their exposure history. We suspect that it would be one of the sources with high attack rates (e.g., Dairy Queen, bakery, or water). Maybe all people, sick or well, use the water and bakery, so that is why these percentages are high. Investigate these three further.
   b. No.
10. a. The investigator used well household members as controls and found no difference in water sources and exposure to Dairy Queen but a big difference between the exposure of victims and the exposure of controls to the North Trail Bakery.
    b. Water history was high in both groups since all members of the same household usually have similar water supply, except possibly in rural areas where wells are used.
11. Milk supply is not the problem because (a) there are no cases among young children, who also receive milk and (b) there is no epidemic in the other counties where the same milk is sold.
12. Figure 1–4 indicates that at lunchtime and again after school a very high percentage of the customers of the bakery are 10 to 19 years old.
13. Yes—all these cases outside the county can be traced to a known exposure to bakery products. As noted in the discussion, two cases were exposed to nothing else from North Trail.
14. The next step is to try to determine the source in the bakery.
15. a. From the curve one can infer that the incubation period is 24 to 28 days.
    b. Yes.

16. Ascertain if the baker's assistant handled bakery products that had un-cooked material. Did the victims consume uncooked bakery material?
17. As usually happens by the time of the investigation, the epidemic is over; there were no signs of active disease in current workers. However, the bakery should be warned about the glazing procedures in order to mini-mize the chance of subsequent problems.
18. SGPT elevation could indicate liver dysfunction, which might indicate a subclinical case of hepatitis.
19. a. Gamma globulin was administered to prevent any secondary spread of hepatitis. There were very few cases after mid May, so use of gamma globulin early in June might have been a little late. However, the epidemic could have been protracted at a low level for several more months through family contacts.
    b. Compare exposed individuals who have and have not received globu-lin in order to determine the number of cases of clinical and subclini-cal hepatitis.

Reference

Tong, J.L., Engle, M., Cullingford, J.S., Shimp, D.T., and Love, C.E. 1962. Am. J. Public Health. 52:976.

Recommended Reading

Mausner, J.S., and Kramer, S. *Mausner and Bahn: Epidemiology—An Introductory Text.* 2d ed. Phila-delphia, W.B. Saunders Co., 1985. Chapter 11 provides a clear discussion of epidemic investigation within the broader context of infectious disease epidemiology.

2

Measures
of Mortality

Objectives Covered

5. Define *crude mortality rate, specific mortality rate* (age, sex, race, and cause), *case fatality rate,* and *proportionate mortality ratio.* Cite one example of the correct use of each of these rates, and interpret statements containing them.
6. Explain what is meant by confounding.
7. State the reasons for adjustment of rates, and interpret statements containing adjusted rates.

Study Notes

Crude mortality rate =

$$\frac{\text{all deaths during a calendar year}}{\text{population at mid year}} \times 1,000 = \text{deaths per 1,000}$$

This crude rate expresses the actual observed mortality rate in a population under study, and it should always be the starting point for further development of adjusted rates.

The crude mortality rate measures the proportion of the population dying every year or the number of deaths in the community per 1,000 population (by convention usually taken as the population at mid year). Because the crude mortality rate is a composite figure reflecting both specific mortality rates and population composition, it is necessary to disentangle these components before meaningful comparisons can be made between population groups. Here the population composition indicated by factors such as age, race, and sex can be regarded as confounding the comparison.

Mortality and Age

Age is the most important characteristic governing mortality. Before the experience of mortality in two populations can be compared, account must be taken of differences in age composition. Crude mortality rates were 10.9 per 1,000 population in Florida in 1981 and 4.4 per 1,000 in Alaska in the same year. The 148% higher mortality rate in Florida is due to its older population, compared with the younger population of Alaska. Mortality comparisons between Alaska and Florida are confounded by the age differences of the two populations.

Confounding is the general term for the effect of a third variable, such as age, on the estimate of the risk of a health outcome, such as mortality, as it relates to a factor of interest, such as locale (Florida vs. Alaska). Confounding occurs whenever a third factor related to the outcome is differently distributed across the levels of the factor of interest. When it occurs, measures must be taken to separate the effect of the confounder from the effect of the factor of interest. Generally, this may be accomplished by selecting subjects to be compared so that they are matched (balanced) with respect to the confounding factor(s) or by using statistical adjustment during analysis to remove the effect of the confounder.

Age-Specific Mortality Rates

Because of the profound effect of age on mortality, it is necessary to construct mortality rates for each age group and to use these rates for comparison. The crude mortality rate and the age-specific mortality rate in Baltimore City are shown in Table 2–1. A paradox is seen. The whites in Baltimore have a higher overall mortality rate than the blacks—15.2 and 9.8, respectively. On the other hand, blacks suffer higher age-specific mortality rates in every age group. What is the explanation for this seeming contradiction? Age distribution is the answer. The population of Baltimore City consists of old whites and young blacks.

Table 2–1 Mortality Rates per 1,000 Population by Age and Race in Baltimore City, 1972

	All Ages	Under 1 Year	1–4	5–17	18–44	45–65	65 and Over
White	15.2	13.5	0.6	0.4	1.5	10.7	59.7
Black	9.8	22.6	1.0	0.5	3.6	18.8	61.1

Source: Baltimore City Statistics.

Age-Adjusted Mortality Rates

When there are differences in age distribution for the groups we wish to compare, age-adjusted rates should be used. To understand what is meant by an age-adjusted rate, it must first be recognized that a crude mortality rate may be expressed as a weighted sum of age-specific mortality rates. Each component of the sum has the following form:

proportion of the population in the age group × age-specific mortality rate

The crude mortality rate is age adjusted by replacing the first term in each of the products by the corresponding age proportion for a standard population (often the U.S. population for a recent year is taken as the standard). This procedure is best illustrated by the following example.

Community A has a population composed of one-half young people and one-half old people. Community B has two-thirds young people and one-third old people in its population. The age-specific death rates in the communities are shown in Table 2–2.

From this information we can determine the crude mortality rates, as follows:

crude mortality rate in A = (1/2)(4) + (1/2)(16) = 10 per 1,000
crude mortality rate in B = (2/3)(5) + (1/3)(20) = 10 per 1,000

Notice that although the probability of dying is lower for A in both age groups, the crude mortality rates are the same. This is because A has an older population than B.

Now we shall adjust the mortality rates for age using a standard population composition of one-third young and two-thirds old, arbitrarily chosen:

age-adjusted mortality rate for A = (1/3)(4) + (2/3)(16) = 12 per 1,000
age-adjusted mortality rate for B = (1/3)(5) + (2/3)(20) = 15 per 1,000

The age-adjusted rates reflect only the probability of dying for the residents of these communities, and thus we have a comparison that is not influenced by the age composition of the populations.

Table 2–2 Age-Specific Mortality Rates per 1,000

Community	Young	Old
A	4	16
B	5	20

In summary, rates are adjusted in order to remove the effect of a confounding factor for which the adjustment is being made. However, it is always necessary first of all to look at the overall crude rates because they represent events. An adjusted rate gives an accurate comparison but does not reveal the underlying raw data, which are shown by the crude rate.

Race- and Sex-Specific Mortality Rates

Males have a higher mortality rate than females. In 1985, the age-adjusted mortality rate per 1,000 for males in the United States was 7.2, whereas for females it was only 4.1. Now, because these rates are age-adjusted, they cannot be explained by age differences and they must relate to sex differences. The male excess holds in both whites and blacks. In whites the rate is 6.9 for males versus 3.9 for females, whereas in blacks it is 10.2 for males versus 5.9 for females. The explanation for the higher overall mortality rate in males lies in the higher rates they suffer in the leading causes of death: cardiovascular and respiratory diseases, cancer, and accidents.

Cause-Specific Mortality Rates

Mortality rates for any specific disease, such as heart disease, may be stated for the entire population or for any age, race, or sex subgroup. Cause-specific mortality rates are computed as

$$\frac{\text{deaths assigned to the specified disease during a calendar year}}{\text{population at mid year}} \times 100,000$$

and so are expressed as deaths per 100,000 population per year (e.g., for diseases of the heart 332 per 100,000 population in the United States in 1985). Diseases of the heart are typical of many diseases in that the death rate shows a differential between the sexes. In order to express these differences more clearly, age-adjusted rates by sex are used so that cause-specific mortality rates are shown as

Diseases of the heart—age-adjusted mortality rates overall and by sex for the United States in 1985, per 100,000 population

Overall, 181
Males, 248
Females, 127

Case Fatality Rate

$$\frac{\text{number of deaths due to the disease in a specified time period}}{\text{number of cases of the disease in the same time period}} \times 100$$

This measure represents the probability of death among diagnosed cases, or the killing power of a disease. It is typically used in acute infectious disease such as acquired immunodeficiency syndrome (AIDS). Its usefulness for chronic diseases (even when, as with tuberculosis, they are infectious) is limited, because the period from onset to death is typically long and variable. The case fatality rate for the same disease may vary in different epidemics as the balance between agent, host, and environment alters.

Proportionate Mortality Ratio (PMR)

This measure is used to demonstrate the proportion of the overall mortality that may be ascribed to a specific cause. Thus, the definition of PMR is

$$\frac{\text{deaths assigned to the disease in a certain year}}{\text{total deaths in the population in the same year}} \times 100$$

The use of this statistic is to display the percentage of deaths due to the cause under study, usually in a certain age and sex group compared with a different age group in the same sex group. For example, white males aged 20 to 24 who have a PMR due to motor vehicle accidents of 40% and a PMR due to ischemic heart disease of 0.3% can be compared with white males aged 50 to 54 who have a PMR due to motor vehicle accidents of 2.7% and a PMR due to ischemic heart disease of 29%. The PMR is often used to emphasize the importance of the contribution of one cause-specific mortality to overall mortality. For example, in 1985 in the United States the PMR of heart disease was 37%. This means that 37% of all deaths, regardless of age, sex, or race, could be ascribed to diseases of the heart, making it, of course, the leading cause of death, with a PMR almost twice that of cancer, which is in second place at 22%. However, note that the statistic tells one nothing about the actual rate involved.

Exercises

1. There were 1,986,000 deaths in the United States in 1982. What additional information is required to compute the crude mortality rate?
2. The crude mortality rate has fluctuated moderately in New York City over the past 40 years, yet the age-adjusted rate has fallen by 42% (Table 2–3). What is the most probable explanation?
3. In 1970, the crude mortality rate (all causes) for Guyana (a developing country in South America) was 6.8 per 1,000 and for the United States it was 9.4 per 1,000.
   a. Can the lower crude mortality rate in Guyana be explained by the fact that the United States has a larger population? Explain your answer.

Table 2–3 Crude and Age-Adjusted Mortality Rates from All Causes per 1,000 Population, New York City and the United States, 1940–1980

Year	New York City		United States	
	Age-Adj.	Crude	Age-Adj.	Crude
1940	11.3	10.2	10.8	10.8
1950	8.9	10.0	8.4	9.6
1960	8.1	11.1	7.6	9.5
1970	7.7	11.2	7.1	9.5
1980	6.6	10.8	5.9	8.9

    b. Give the most probable explanation for the lower crude mortality rate in Guyana.

4. Crude and age-adjusted mortality rates (per 100,000 people) from "arteriosclerotic and degenerative heart diseases" are shown for Chile and the United States for 1967 (Table 2–4). Which of the two rates is preferable for comparing the mortality rate from heart disease in the two countries? Why? Why do the ratios of the crude and age-adjusted rates for the two countries differ?

5. A city contains 100,000 people (45,000 males and 55,000 females), and 1,000 people die per year (600 males and 400 females). There were 50 cases (40 males and 10 females) of lung cancer per year, of whom 45 died (36 males and 9 females). Compute:
    a. Crude mortality rate
    b. Sex-specific mortality rate
    c. Cause-specific mortality rate for lung cancer
    d. Case fatality rate for lung cancer
    e. PMR for lung cancer

Table 2–4 Crude and Age-Adjusted Mortality Rates from Arteriosclerotic and Degenerative Heart Diseases

	Crude Rates	Age-Adjusted Rates
Chile	67.4	58.2
United States	316.3	131.4
Ratio, United States: Chile	4.7	2.3

Exercise Answers

1. The total U.S. mid-year population in 1982, which was estimated to be 230,930,230. This gives a crude mortality rate of

$$\frac{1,986,000}{230,930,230} \times 1,000 = 8.6 \text{ per } 1,000$$

2. The crude mortality rate is not the best measure of trends in mortality since it assumes a stable age composition in the population. The age composition of New York City has changed over the past 40 years, with an increasing proportion of the population being in the older age groups. An age-adjusted rate should be used for comparison, which shows a steady fall. Similar patterns are found in U.S. mortality rates.

3. a. The fact that the population of the United States is larger than that of Guyana cannot explain a difference in rates, since the mortality rate refers to number of deaths per 1,000 population in both countries.

   b. Age-specific mortality rates are higher in Guyana, but the population in Guyana is younger. High age-specific death rates in the first decades of life, typical of developing countries, can lead to a relatively young population, because comparatively few people survive to live to an old age, thus giving a relative deficiency of old people. Thus, paradoxically, the crude mortality rate in developing countries is low, despite high age-specific mortality rates, because of the small proportion of elderly persons.

4. Age-adjusted rates are preferable. Crude mortality rates reflect not only age-specific mortality rates but also the age composition of the population. Since Chile, like Guyana, has a younger population than the United States, age-adjusted rates are needed for comparing the risk of death from heart disease in the two countries. When differences in age composition are removed by the adjustment, the mortality rate from heart disease in the United States is only 2.3 times that of Chile, rather than 4.7.

5. a. $1,000/100,000 \times 1000 = 10$ per 1,000.

   b. $600/45,000 \times 1000 = 13.3$ per 1,000 for males.

      $400/55,000 \times 1000 = 7.3$ per 1,000 for females.

   c. $45/100,000 \times 1000 = 0.45$ per 1,000.

   d. $45/50 \times 100 = 90\%$.

   e. $45/1,000 \times 100 = 4.5\%$.

Recommended Readings

Hennekens, C.H., and Buring, J.E. *Epidemiology in Medicine.* Edited by S. L. Mayrent. Boston, Little, Brown, & Co., 1987. Chapter 12 is an excellent presentation of the concept of confounding and the methods to overcome the problem.

Lilienfeld, D.E., and Stolley P.D. *Foundations of Epidemiology,* 3rd ed. New York, Oxford University Press, 1994. Chapters 4 and 5 provide an introduction to mortality statistics and their role in epidemiologic investigation.

Mausner, J.S., and Kramer, S. *Mausner and Bahn: Epidemiology—An Introductory Text.* 2d ed. Philadelphia, W.B. Saunders Co., 1985. Chapters 3 through 5 present the sources of mortality data, the common rates used to assess mortality risk, and the major sources of bias.

3

Incidence and Prevalence

Objectives Covered

8. Define *incidence* and *prevalence;* state the relationship between them.
9. Name the factors that may cause variation in each measurement. Give the uses of each rate.

Study Notes

Incidence and *prevalence* are the two major measures of disease frequency.

Incidence rates are designed to measure the rate at which people without a disease develop the disease during a specific period of time, that is, the number of *new* cases of a disease in a population over a period of time. Prevalence rates measure the number of people in a population who have the disease at a given point in time. These rates are defined as follows:

$$\frac{\text{incidence}}{\text{rate}} = \frac{\text{number of new cases of a disease over a period of time}}{\text{population at risk of the disease in the time period}}$$

$$\frac{\text{prevalence}}{\text{rate}} = \frac{\text{total number of cases of a disease at a given time}}{\text{total population at risk at a given time}}$$

The time referred to in the numerator of the prevalence rate may be a period of time such as a year or a specific time point such as January 1, 1984. In the former case, the term *period prevalence* is used, while in the latter it is *point prevalence.*

Incidence measures the appearance of disease; prevalence measures the existence of disease.

Incidence means *new.*

Prevalence means *all.*

Incidence reflects only the rate of disease occurrence. A change in incidence means there is a change in the balance of etiological factors, either some naturally occurring fluctuation or possibly the application of an effective prevention program. Incidence is of importance to the researcher seeking etiology.

Prevalence, however, depends on two factors: the incidence and the duration of disease. Thus, a change in disease prevalence may reflect a change in incidence or outcome or both. For example, improvements in therapy, by preventing death but at the same time not producing recovery, may give rise to the apparently paradoxical effect of an increase in prevalence of the disease. Decrease in prevalence may result not only from a decrease in incidence but also from a shortening of the duration of disease through either more rapid recovery or more rapid death. Furthermore, if duration decreased sufficiently, a decrease in prevalence could take place despite an increase in incidence. The level of prevalence (all cases) is increased by incidence (new cases) and decreased by recovery and death (Figure 3–1).

Prevalence is the product of incidence times duration. This relationship is most apparent in a stable, chronic disease. In this case the incidence may be derived, provided the prevalence and duration are known.

Prevalence is used by health planners because it measures the need for treatment and hospital beds and aids in planning health facilities and manpower needs. Prevalence may be determined by a single survey; by contrast, incidence rates are difficult to measure. A defined population, initially free of the disease in question,

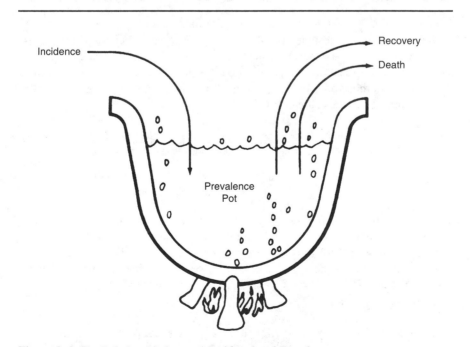

Figure 3–1 The Relationship between Incidence and Prevalence

must be followed for a period of time in order to ascertain the rate of appearance of new cases. Incidence rates are used to make statements about the probability or risk of disease. Incidence rates of disease are compared among population groups with different exposures or attributes in order to measure the influence such factors may have on the occurrence of disease.

Number of persons

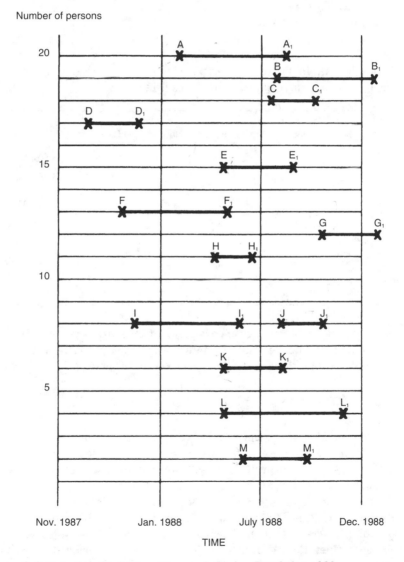

Figure 3–2 Episodes of Infectious Mononucleosis in a Population of 20

Exercises

1. Each heavy black line between the Xs on Figure 3–2 represents an episode of infectious mononucleosis, and each line represents a person (so that there is a defined population of 20). For 1988 compute, for mononucleosis
   a. the incidence
   b. the period prevalence
   Assume a survey is conducted in July 1988; what point prevalence will result?
2. From the data in Table 3–1, compute the average duration, in years, of the five chronic neurological conditions listed.

Table 3–1 Prevalence and Incidence of Selected Neurological Diseases in Rochester, Minnesota

$$P = I \times D$$
$$376 = 38.8 \times D$$

Disease	Rates per 100,000 Population	
	Prevalence	Incidence
Epilepsy	376	30.8
Multiple sclerosis	55	5.0
Parkinson's disease	157	20.0
Motor neuron disease	7	1.7
Central nervous system neoplasms	69	17.3

3. Assume that the prevalence of coronary heart disease decreases after age 70, while its incidence continues to increase with age. What is the most probable explanation for the divergence of these rates?

Exercise Answers

1. a. 10/20 or 50%. (The episode $J–J_1$ is counted as contributing to incidence in 1988; although it appears to be a reinfection.)
   b. 10 new + 1 old = prevalent cases/20 population. The period prevalence in 1988 = 11/20 = 55%.
   Point prevalence in July = 5 cases/20 population = 25%.
2. Epilepsy—12.2; multiple sclerosis—11; Parkinson's disease—7.8; motor neuron disease—4.1; central nervous system neoplasms—4.0.
3. Patients older than age 70 who develop coronary heart disease have shorter survival times than the younger patients.

Recommended Readings

Fletcher, R.H., Fletcher, S.W., and Wagner, E.H. *Clinical Epidemiology: The Essentials.* Baltimore, Williams & Wilkins, 1988. Chapter 4 is a discussion of measures of disease frequency in a clinical framework.

Lilienfeld, D.W., and Stolley P.D. *Foundations of Epidemiology,* 3rd ed. New York, Oxford University Press, 1994. Chapters 4 through 7 provide an introduction to mortality and morbidity statistics and their role in epidemiologic investigation.

Mausner, J.S., and Kramer, S. *Mausner and Bahn: Epidemiology—An Introductory Text.* 2d ed. Philadelphia, W.B. Saunders Co., 1985. Chapters 3 through 5 present the major community indices of health, their sources, and the major sources of bias.

4

Measures of Risk

Objectives Covered

10. Define *absolute risk, relative risk,* and *attributable risk,* and interpret statements that employ these terms.
11. Explain what is meant by effect modification.

Study Notes

Relative and Attributable Risk

Relative and attributable risk are two measures of the association between exposure to a particular factor and risk of a certain outcome:

$$\text{relative risk} = \frac{\text{incidence rate among exposed}}{\text{incidence rate among nonexposed}}$$

$$\text{attributable risk} = \text{incidence rate among exposed} - \text{incidence rate among nonexposed}$$

Attributable risk is also sometimes expressed as the preventive fraction among the exposed, that is,

$$\frac{\text{incidence rate among exposed} - \text{incidence rate among nonexposed}}{\text{incidence rate among exposed}} \times 100$$

The absolute risk is synonymous with incidence and means the rate of occurrence of the condition or disease. It is the basic rate from which relative and attributable risk are derived. The clinician uses the relative risk, which expresses the risk of one group with a factor (e.g., males, hypertensives, cigarette smokers) compared with the risk of a reference group without such a factor (e.g., females, normotensives, nonsmokers). Relative risk is the ratio of the incidence of the group with the factor to the incidence of the group without the factor. If the factor is smoking, it tells the clinician how much the risk for a patient who smokes is increased compared with a nonsmoker. Such a patient may be in a high-risk group for a disease (by virtue of smoking), and a screening test might be indicated to detect early asymptomatic disease. Factors associated with disease by virtue of elevated relative risks are termed *risk factors*. The relative risk indicates the benefit that might accrue to the patient if the risk factor is removed; that is, it measures the decrease in risk to be anticipated for the sacrifice involved in behavior change (stopping smoking).

The relative risk does not measure the probability that someone with the factor will develop the disease. For example, if the relative risk associated with the presence of the factor is 10, this merely means that the probability for the disease is 10 times higher than in someone without the factor. The individual with the factor might still have a very remote chance of getting the disease, if the disease is rare. It has been shown, for example, that women who have used oral contraceptives for a long time have a high relative risk of developing liver cell adenoma. However, the underlying incidence of this disease is so small that the increased risk assumed by the users is insignificant in comparison to the benefits gained. It is especially important to bear this point in mind when the relative risk has been determined from a retrospective study (see Chapter 12). This is because this design does not yield incidence rates for either the exposed or the nonexposed groups. Thus, the relative risk estimate for those exposed is merely a multiple of an unknown incidence rate among those not exposed.

Relative risk also measures the strength of an association between a factor and a certain outcome; thus, a high relative risk points toward causation and is useful in research for the etiology of disease.

Attributable risk measures the amount of the absolute risk (incidence) that can be attributed to one particular factor (i.e., smoking). It is computed by taking the incidence rate of the group with the factor (smokers) and subtracting the rate for the group without the factor (nonsmokers). The excess suffered by the smokers is the attributable risk due to smoking. As defined above, the attributable risk indicates the excess of disease due to a factor in that subgroup of the population that is exposed to the factor. If we replace "incidence rate among exposed" in the formula for attributable risk with "incidence rate in the total population," we have the population attributable risk. The population attributable risk is generally of significance to public health authorities, since it measures the potential benefit to be expected if the exposure could be reduced in the population.

Clinical Implications

Although a factor may have a high relative risk, with reference to a common outcome or disease, if that factor is found only rarely in the population, the impact on the population will be small. For example, patients with familial multiple polyposis have a high relative risk for cancer of the large bowel, with a relative risk greater than 20 (i.e., they are more than 20 times as likely to develop large bowel cancer than those without familial polyposis), but the incidence of large bowel cancer due to familial multiple polyposis is very small because the attribute is rare. Therefore, it is necessary that a factor both have a high relative risk and be prevalent in the population in order for it to influence the incidence of the disease in the population.

Risk estimates are probability statements, and it must be remembered that (1) all those exposed to the factor do not develop the disease but merely have an increased probability of doing so and (2) some who have not been exposed to the factor will develop the disease.

Effect Modification

Age does not always act as a confounder; it can act to modify the relationship between a risk factor and disease. That is, the risk factor under study has one relationship at young ages and another at older ages. In this case, age acts in concert with the risk factor (degree of relationship) to help determine risk. The important distinction between age as a confounder and age as an effect modifier is whether the age-specific relative risks or risk ratios change appreciably, by more than chance would dictate. Finding such evidence of effect modification can have important implications for the understanding of disease etiology.

The study of the Li-Fraumeni Syndrome by Strong et al., provides an example. In this study, primary and secondary relatives of 3-year survivors of childhood soft-tissue sarcoma diagnosed between 1944–1976 at University of Texas M.D. Anderson Cancer Center were queried for diagnoses of invasive malignancies.

Table 4–1 Observed and Expected Relatives with Cancer of 159 3-Year Survivors of Childhood Soft-Tissue Sarcoma Diagnosed between 1944 and 1976 at the University of Texas M.D. Anderson Cancer Center, Houston, Texas

Relationship by Age	N of Relatives	Standardized Incidence Ratio	95% Confidence Interval
First-degree relatives	758	1.64	1.14–2.30
Age <35 yrs		2.90	1.50–5.07
Age 35–74 yrs		1.32	Not significant
Second-degree relatives	1,693	0.80	0.67–0.94
Age <35 yrs		0.92	Not significant
Age 35–74 yrs		0.78	0.65–0.03
Total		0.88	Not significant

Source: Adapted from Strong LC, et al., 1992.

The results were compared with the number of such malignancies expected by type based on the age-, sex-, calendar year–specific experience of the Connecticut Tumor Registry. Table 4–1 shows the results of these analyses by degree of relationship to the childhood sarcoma survivor and age. The standardized incidence ratio or ratio of observed to expected cancers indicates that the only large and statistically significant increase in cancers occurs in young primary relatives of the sarcoma survivors. The finding of an increased risk of rare cancers among young, close relatives of childhood sarcoma cases, along with other evidence was used to support the hypothesis of genetic predisposition to cancer in such families. Further genetic and biochemical studies have supported the conclusion that a mutation of the p53 tumor suppressor gene inherited through autosomal dominant transmission in susceptible families may be responsible for these unusual findings.

Exercises

1. **From the data in Table 4-2, compute**
   a. **relative risk of smokers versus nonsmokers**
   b. **attributable risk for smokers**

Table 4–2 Death Rates from Lung Cancer in People Aged 35 or Older

	Death Rates, from Lung Cancer, per 1,000 People Aged 35 or Older, per Year
Nonsmokers	0.07
Cigarette smokers	0.96

2. **Explain your answers to (a) and (b) above in narrative form.**
3. **What are the uses of relative risk**
   a. **to the clinician?**
   b. **to the researcher?**
4. **What are the uses of attributable risk**
   a. **to the physician responsible for prevention programs?**
   b. **to the physician responsible for health planning for large groups?**
5. a. **What does absolute risk measure?**
   b. **When is it used?**
6. **Males aged 35 who are heavy cigarette smokers have a relative risk for lung cancer of 14. Compute the probability of a male cigarette smoker aged 35 developing lung cancer per year.**

Exercise Answers

1. a. 0.96/0.07 = 13.7.
   b. 0.96 – 0.07 = 0.89.
2. a. Cigarette smokers older than 35 years of age are 13.7 times more likely to die of lung cancer than nonsmokers.
   b. Of the overall rate of deaths from lung cancer in cigarette smokers (0.96), 0.89 is attributable to cigarette smoking, or the percent attributable risk of lung cancer due to cigarette smoking is 0.89/0.96 × 100 = 93%.
3. a. Relative risk tells the clinician the size of the excess risk that the patient with exposure to a factor (i.e., hypertension, high serum cholesterol) runs, compared with a patient without exposure to such a factor. Relative risk enables the clinician to identify patients at high risk of certain outcomes. It does not provide the clinician with the absolute risk.
   b. The relative risk measures the strength of an association; thus a high relative risk suggests etiology or causality.
4. a. Attributable risk measures the impact that removal of a certain factor may have on the incidence of disease; therefore, prevention programs can be justified on the basis of a large attributable risk.
   b. Identification of attributable risks for various exposures in certain diseases aids in rational planning for health services.
5. a. It measures incidence, or rate of occurrence.
   b. It is used in actuarial or predictive situations.
6. Given the relative risk alone, it is impossible to compute such a rate. If it is known, however, that the absolute risk (incidence) for males (nonsmokers) aged 35 for lung cancer is 0.1/1,000, then the incidence for heavy cigarette smokers is 0.1 × 14, or 1.4/1,000.

Reference

Strong, L.C., Williams, W.R., and Transky, N.A. 1992. The Li-Fraumeni syndrome: From clinical epidemiology to molecular genetics. Am. J. Epidemiol. 135:190-9.

Recommended Readings

Fletcher, R.H., Fletcher, S.W., and Wagner, E.H. *Clinical Epidemiology: The Essentials.* Baltimore, Williams & Wilkins, 1988. Chapter 5 is a clear and concise presentation of the concept of risk, how it is assessed, and how it is interpreted.

Hennekens, C.H., and Buring, J.E. *Epidemiology in Medicine.* Edited by S.L. Mayrent. Boston, Little, Brown, & Co., 1987. Chapter 4 focuses on the computation and interpretation of risk.

Self-Assessment 1

Objectives Covered: 1–11

Best Choice—Select One Answer Only

An outbreak of gastritis occurred on a cruise ship. The data in Table A1–1 were obtained, shortly after the outbreak, from a questionnaire completed by everyone on board the ship.

Table A1–1 Data from an Outbreak of Gastritis on a Cruise Ship

Food	People Who Ate Food		People Who Did Not Eat	
	Sick	Well	Sick	Well
Herring	200	800	100	900
Chicken	650	350	100	900
Spinach souffle	200	800	500	500
Oysters	300	700	400	600
Chocolate mousse	600	400	450	550

Use these data for questions 1 and 2.

1. What is the most likely infective food on the cruise ship?
   a. herring
   b. chicken
   c. spinach souffle
   d. oysters
   e. chocolate mousse
2. What is the relative risk of developing gastritis for herring consumption?
   a. 0.5
   b. 2.0
   c. 2.3
   d. 8.0
3. California Highway Patrol statistics revealed that more accidents occurred to blue cars than to cars of any other color. The inference that while driving a

39

blue car, one is at higher risk of accident than while driving a car of another color is
   a. correct
   b. incorrect, because the comparison is not based on rates
   c. incorrect, because no control or comparison group is used
   d. incorrect, because no test of statistical significance has been made
   e. incorrect, because prevalence is used instead of incidence
4. In a study of 500 cases of a disease and 500 controls, the suspected etiological factor is found in 400 of the cases and 100 of the controls. The absolute risk (incidence) of disease in people with the factor is
   a. 80%
   b. 40%
   c. 16%
   d. 20%
   e. cannot be computed from data given
5. In 1945, 1,000 women worked in a factory painting radium dials on watches. The incidence of bone cancer in these women up to 1975 was compared with that of 1,000 women who worked as telephone operators in 1945. Twenty of the radium dial workers and four of the telephone operators developed bone cancer between 1945 and 1975. The relative risk of developing bone cancer for radium dial workers is $4/20$
   a. 2
   b. 4
   c. 5
   d. 8
   e. cannot be computed from the data given
6. *Epidemic* refers to
   a. a disease that has a low rate of occurrence but that is constantly present in a community or region
   b. an attack rate in excess of 10 per 1,000 population
   c. the occurrence of illnesses of similar nature clearly in excess of the normal expectation for that population at that time
   d. diseases of the respiratory system that occur seasonally
   e. the annual case rate per 100,000 population
7. When a new treatment is developed that prevents death but does not produce recovery from a disease, the following will occur:
   a. Prevalence of the disease will decrease.
   b. Incidence of the disease will increase.
   c. Prevalence of the disease will increase.
   d. Incidence of the disease will decrease.
   e. Incidence and prevalence of the disease will decrease.

Regionville is a community of 100,000 persons. During 1985, there were 1,000 deaths from all causes. All cases of tuberculosis have been found, and they total 300: 200 males and 100 females. During 1985, there were 60 deaths from tuberculosis, 50 of them in males.

Use the above data for questions 8 through 12.

8. Crude mortality rate in Regionville is
    a. 300 per 100,000
    b. 60 per 1,000
    c. 10 per 1,000
    d. 100 per 1,000
    e. cannot be computed from data given
9. The proportionate mortality due to tuberculosis is
    a. 20%
    b. 30%
    c. 6%
    d. 3%
    e. cannot be computed from the data given
10. The case fatality rate for tuberculosis is
    a. 6%
    b. 20%
    c. 2%
    d. equal in males and females
    e. cannot be computed from data given
11. The cause-specific mortality rate for tuberculosis is
    a. 60 per 100,000
    b. 300 per 100,000
    c. 200 per 1,000
    d. 20%
    e. cannot be computed from data given
12. The sex-specific mortality rate for tuberculosis in males is
    a. 0.5 per 1,000
    b. 25%
    c. greater in males than females
    d. cannot be computed from data given
13. Communities P and Q have equal age-adjusted mortality rates. Community P has a lower crude mortality rate than Q. One may conclude that
    a. The two communities have identical age distributions.
    b. Diagnosis is more accurate in P than Q.
    c. P has an older population than Q.

d. Diagnosis is less accurate in Q than P.

e. P has a younger population than Q.

14. Table A1–2 shows the sex distribution in three large series of cases of a disease.

Table A1–2 Sex Distribution in Three Series of Cases of a Disease

Series	Male Cases	Female Cases
1	200	100
2	250	50
3	450	150
Total	900	300

The incidence rate of this disease by sex was

a. twice as great in males as in females

b. three times greater in males than in females

c. five times greater in males than in females

d. from two to five times as great in males as in females

e. cannot be computed from the data given

Table A1–3 shows data from a large study of bladder cancer and cigarette smoking in Boston.

Table A1–3 Bladder Cancer Rates in Cigarette Smokers and Nonsmokers

	Bladder Cancer Rates per 100,000 Males
Cigarette smokers	48.0
Nonsmokers	25.4

Use these data for questions 15 and 16.

15. The relative risk of developing bladder cancer for male cigarette smokers compared with male nonsmokers is

a. 48.0

b. $48.0 - 25.4 = 22.6$

c. $48.0/25.4 = 1.89$

d. $\dfrac{48.0 - 25.4}{48.0}$

e. cannot be computed from the data given

16. The attributable risk of bladder cancer due to cigarette smoking in male cigarette smokers is
    a. 48.0/25.4 = 1.89
    b. 48.0 – 25.4 = 22.6 per 100,000
    c. 48.0
    d. 48.0/100,00 = 0.00048
    e. cannot be computed from these data

Table A1–4 shows the total number of people who ate each of the two specified food items possibly infective with group A streptococci. Table A1–5 shows the number of sick people (e.g., those with acute sore throats) who ate each of the various specified combinations of the food items.

Table A1–4 Total Number of People Who Ate Each Specified Combination of Food Items

	Ate Pheasant	Did Not Eat Pheasant
Ate caviar	100	100
Did not eat caviar	100	100

Table A1–5 Number of Sick People Who Ate Each Specified Combination of Food Items

	Ate Pheasant	Did Not Eat Pheasant
Ate caviar	50	20
Did not eat caviar	50	25

Use these data for questions 17 and 18.

17. What is the sore throat attack rate in people who ate both pheasant and caviar?
    a. 50/50
    b. 50/70
    c. 50/75
    d. 50/100
    e. 50/200

18. According to the results shown in Tables A1–4 and A1–5, which of the following food items (or combination of food items) is (are) most likely to be the infective item(s):
    a. pheasant only
    b. caviar only
    c. neither pheasant nor caviar
    d. both pheasant and caviar
    e. cannot be calculated from data given

19. Which of the following health statistics would be most useful in selecting risk factors to target for intervention in order to have the greatest health impact? (Assume the planned interventions are equally effective but resources are limited.)
    a. incidence of the disease among the exposed
    b. attributable risk
    c. prevalence of the disease among the exposed
    d. relative risk of the disease
    e. proportionate mortality

20. In order to assess how strongly related an exposure is to a disease, which would be the best health statistic?
    a. incidence of the disease among the exposed
    b. attributable risk
    c. prevalence of the exposure
    d. relative risk
    e. proportionate mortality

21. Referring to Tables A1–2, A1–4, and A1–5, which of the following are correct statements regarding confounding?
    1. Eating or not eating potatoes and gravy is a confounder when assessing the risk of infection associated with eating turkey.
    2. Eating or not eating caviar is a confounder when assessing the risk of infection associated with eating pheasant.
    a. 1 is true, but 2 is not
    b. 2 is true, but 1 is not
    c. both 1 and 2 are true
    d. neither 1 nor 2 is true
    e. cannot assess confounding on the basis of information given

22. The relative risk of ischemic stroke for non-whites compared with whites is about 2 for those aged 35 to 64 years and about 1 for those 65 years of age and above. This is best described as
    a. confounding of the effect of race by age
    b. modification of the effect of race by age
    c. elimination of the effect of race by age-adjustment
    d. elimination of the effect of age by race-adjustment
    e. all of the above

K-Type Questions

Key

a	b	c	d	e
1, 2, 3	1 and 3	2 and 4	only 4	all 4
are correct	are correct	are correct	is correct	are correct

23. One hundred twelve persons became ill following, and apparently as a result of, a picnic at which 250 persons were in attendance, including 80 men and 170 women. Of those who became ill, 76 were females and 36 were males.
    1. The sex-specific attack rate for males was 0.32.
    2. The sex-specific attack rate for males was 0.45.
    3. The sex-specific attack rate for females was 0.68.
    4. The overall attack rate was 0.45.
    Note: 36/112 = 0.32
    36/250 = 0.14
    36/80 = 0.45
    112/250 = 0.45
    72/112 = 0.68
    76/250 = 0.30
    76/170 = 0.45

24. Five years after the introduction of a vigorous detection and treatment program, the prevalence of diabetes mellitus was found to be greater than in the year prior to the introduction of the program. Which of the following are possible reasons?
    1. an increase in previously undetected cases
    2. a reduction in the risk factors predisposing to diabetes
    3. a decrease in case fatality rate of diabetes
    4. an increase in the proportionate mortality of diabetes

---

Table A1–6 Patient Mortality by Age in Two Urban Hospitals in 1988

Age (yr)	Hospital A			Hospital B		
	Deaths	Patients	Death Rate per 1,000	Deaths	Patients	Death Rate per 1,000
<50	10	500	20	30	1000	30
>49	50	1000	50	30	500	60
Totals	60	1500		60	1500	

25. Which of the following are correct interpretations of Table A1–6?
    1. The crude mortality rates are equal in hospitals A and B.
    2. The age-specific mortality rates are greater in hospital B.
    3. Hospital A draws an older patient population.
    4. The age-adjusted mortality rate would be greater in hospital B.

5

Biological Variability

Objectives Covered

12. State the purpose of a frequency distribution and cumulative frequency distribution in describing a set of biological measurements.
13. Define *mean, median, mode,* and *percentile,* and describe the features of a distribution that each characterizes.
14. Contrast the features of a normal (Gaussian) distribution to those of a skewed distribution.
15. Explain why the mean ±2 standard deviations is often used to establish the "normal range" and what practical difficulties might be encountered using this procedure in clinical practice.

Study Notes

Variation is inherent in all observed data. Biological measurements, however, are particularly susceptible to variability—from one individual to another, within one individual from one occasion to another, from one observer to another, etc. To study biological data we need statistical techniques that will help us cope with such variability.

Frequency Distributions

The frequency distribution, as presented in tabular or graphic form, provides a way of organizing a collection or sample of measurements so that we can determine what levels are common and what levels are rare. An example of a frequency distribution table is shown in Table 5–1. Such a table is developed by grouping the data according to well-defined classes (as shown in the first column of Table 5–1) and recording the number in each class (as shown in the second column). Thus, the first two columns in Table 5–1 give the frequency distribution of serum uric acid

Table 5–1 Distribution of Serum Uric Acid Levels (267 Healthy Male Blood Donors)

Uric Acid (mg/dl)	Number of Men	Percent of Total	Cumulative Percent of Total
3.0–3.4	2	0.8	0.8
3.5–3.9	15	5.6	6.4
4.0–4.4	33	12.4	18.7
4.5–4.9	40	15.0	33.7
5.0–5.4	54	20.2	53.9
5.5–5.9	47	17.6	71.5
6.0–6.4	38	14.2	85.8
6.5–6.9	16	6.0	91.8
7.0–7.4	15	5.6	97.4
7.5–7.9	3	1.1	98.5
8.0–8.4	1	0.4	98.9
8.5–8.9	3	1.1	100.0

for the 267 male blood donors. By dividing the number in the class by the total number we obtain the relative frequency, as is shown in the third column of Table 5–1, expressed as a percent. Notice that this column gives the distribution in a standard form, and it may now be compared with similar samples that may differ in size. The fourth column gives the cumulative frequency distribution, which enables us to make a quantitative statement about a given level of the measurement. For example, we can say that about 92% of the individuals in Table 5–1 have uric acid levels below 7 mg/dl.

A graphic display of the frequency distribution is shown in Figure 5–1. This graph is called a histogram. A plot of the cumulative frequency distribution, as shown in Figure 5–2, is useful for determining percentiles of the distribution. A percentile is the level of the measurement below which a specified proportion of the distribution falls. For example, from Figure 5–2 we find that 25% of the distribution falls below a uric acid level of 4.7 mg/dl; 4.7 mg/dl is thus the 25th percentile of that distribution.

Indices of Central Tendency

It is often desirable to have an index that indicates the typical experience for a group. This index would therefore locate the center of the frequency distribution. The *mode, median,* and *mean* are three indices of central tendency:

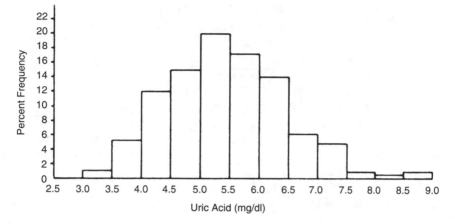

Figure 5–1 Histogram of Serum Uric Acid Distribution in 267 Healthy Males

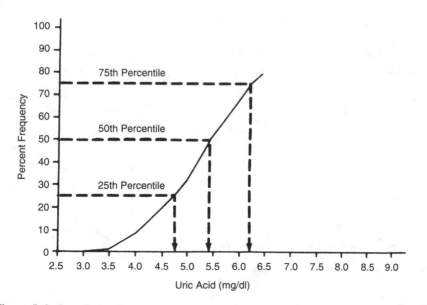

Figure 5–2 Cumulative Frequency Plot

mode = the most frequently occurring observation

median = that measurement level below which half the observations fall, the 50th percentile

$$\text{mean} = \frac{\text{sum of the observed measurements}}{\text{number of observations}}$$

For any symmetrical distribution, the mean, median, and mode will be identical. With a skewed distribution, however, these indices will be arranged as shown in Figure 5–3, with the mean being the most distorted by extreme observations. The distribution on the right (B) is said to be positively skewed because its longer tail is in the positive direction.

Indices of Variation

In addition to describing the central tendency it is often desirable to describe the amount of variation present in a collection of measurements. An easy way of doing this is to determine the range, the difference between the highest and the lowest observations. However, because of its mathematical properties, the standard deviation is a much more useful index of variation. The standard deviation is a measure of the average distance of the observations from their mean. Its use in the interpretation of data relates mainly to its role as a parameter of the normal distribution.

The Normal Distribution Curve

The normal (or Gaussian) distribution curve is a theoretical model that has been found to fit many naturally occurring phenomena. To make use of this model we

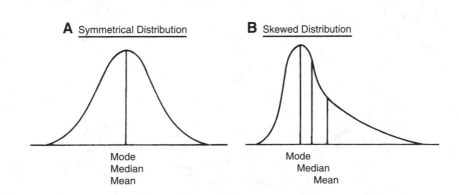

Figure 5–3 Indices of Central Tendency for Symmetrical and Skewed Distributions

need only have knowledge of the mean and the standard deviation, denoted by μ and σ, respectively. The normal distribution curve has a bell-shaped appearance, symmetrical about the mean, with approximately 95% of its relative frequency in the interval $\mu \pm 2\sigma$ (Figure 5–4). It can also be stated that $\mu \pm \sigma$ includes approximately 68% and $\mu \pm 3\sigma$ includes almost all of the distribution (99.7%).

The Normal Range

It has become common practice in medicine to take as "normal limits" the 2.5th and the 97.5th percentiles of the distribution of the measurement for a healthy population. If it can be assumed that the distribution follows the normal curve, then these limits may be expressed as

normal limits = mean $\pm$ 2 standard deviations

If the distribution is severely skewed, however, then the 2.5th and 97.5th percentiles should be determined in another way. One approach would be to find them on a cumulative frequency plot, such as that shown in Figure 5–2.

Exercises

Pediatric Serum Cholesterol

Serum cholesterol levels were obtained for 2,033 patients of a pediatrician in Scottsdale, Arizona (Friedman and Goldberg, 1973). This pediatric population was described by the authors as white, middle-class children from a suburban community. Blood samples were obtained by fingerstick at the pediatrician's office. The cumulative distributions shown in Figure 5–5 summarize the data gathered.

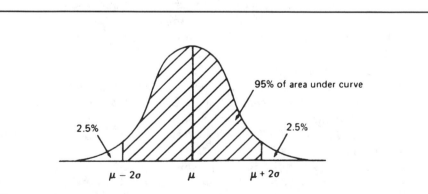

Figure 5–4 Normal Distribution Curve

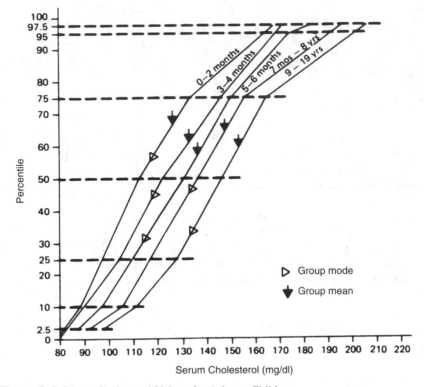

Figure 5–5 Serum Cholesterol Values for Arizona Children

---

1. **What percentage of the children between seven months and eight years of age had cholesterol levels above 120 mg/dl?**
2. **What is the median cholesterol level for children between the ages of 9 and 19 years?**
3. **What serum cholesterol value would you use to identify children two months of age and younger with levels in the highest 5%?**
4. **Which of the children listed below in Table 5–2 would you classify as abnormal on the basis of serum cholesterol?**
5. **What does Figure 5–5 tell you about serum cholesterol and its relationship with age?**
6. **From the cumulative distributions given in Figure 5–5, what can you tell about the shapes of the age-specific frequency distributions for serum cholesterol?**

7. **Why is it better to use the cumulative distribution to obtain normal limits for pediatric serum cholesterol than to use the rule of the mean ± 2 standard deviations?**

Table 5–2 Serum Cholesterol Values for Eight Children

Patient	Age	Serum Cholesterol (mg/dl)
Amy S.	3 years	164
George C.	4 months	183
Kerry H.	3 weeks	150
David H.	5 years	138
Julie K.	12 years	185
Gary M.	1 month	180
Laura V.	7 years	182

Blood Lead and Serum Urea

Raised blood lead concentrations have been investigated for a possible association with renal insufficiency (Campbell et al., 1977). Distributions of blood lead for 54 subjects with raised serum urea and 54 controls matched for age and sex are shown in Figure 5–6. The mean, median, and mode for each group are shown in Table 5–3.

8. **How would you describe the shape of each distribution?**
9. **What do the measures of central tendency tell you about the shape of the two distributions?**
10. **When a distribution is of the type shown for subjects with raised urea, the mean is a somewhat misleading indication of the typical level in the group. Why?**

Table 5–3 Measures of Central Tendency (μmol/liter)

	Subjects with Raised Serum Urea	Controls
Mean	1.73	1.33
Median	1.44	1.31
Mode	1.25	1.25

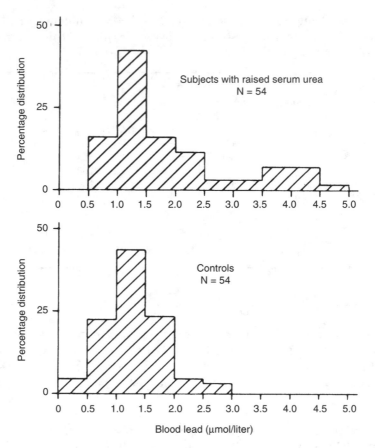

Figure 5–6 Distribution of Blood Lead Levels in People with Raised Serum Urea Concentrations [> 6.6 µmol/liter (39.8 mg/dl)] and Age and Sex-Matched Controls

Exercise Answers

1. **70%.**
2. **145 mg/dl.**
3. **165 mg/dl.**
4. **Taking the 2.5th and 97.5th percentiles as normal limits, we would classify George C. and Gary M. as having abnormal cholesterol levels.**
5. **There is an increase in cholesterol level with age. This increase is especially pronounced early in life.**

6. They are positively skewed. This is evident from the fact that in almost every age group the mean is higher than the median, which in turn is higher than the mode.

7. Since the distributions are skewed, normal limits given by the rule of the mean ± 2 standard deviations would not represent the 2.5th and 97.5th percentiles.

8. The distribution for subjects with raised urea levels is positively skewed while that for controls is nearly symmetrical.

9. The relationship of the three measures confirms the answer given for 8. For the group with raised serum urea levels, the mean is appreciably higher than the median, which in turn is higher than the mode. This is characteristic of a positively skewed distribution. All three measures of central tendency are nearly the same for the control group and thus indicate a symmetrical distribution.

10. This is because it is distorted by the few subjects with extremely high blood levels. When the distribution is skewed, this effect is not balanced by an equal effect at the other extreme. The median is most often used in this type of situation because it still has a clear interpretation.

References

Campbell, B.C., Beattie, A.D., Moore, M.R., Goldberg, A., and Reid, A.G. 1977. Renal insufficiency associated with excessive lead exposure. Br. Med. J. 482:485.

Friedman, G., and Goldberg, S.J. 1973. Normal serum cholesterol values. JAMA 225:610.

Recommended Readings

Bland, M. *An Introduction to Medical Statistics.* Oxford, Oxford Medical Publications, 1987. Chapter 4 is a clear and concise description of the basic methods used for summarizing data.

Ingelfinger, J.A., Mosteller, F., Thibodeau, L.A., and Ware, J.H. *Biostatistics in Clinical Medicine.* New York, McGraw-Hill Inc., 1994. The relevance of frequency distributions and variability to clinical problems are discussed in Chapters 5 and 5A.

6
Probability

Objectives Covered

16. Determine probabilities from frequency distributions.
17. Explain what is meant by conditional probability.
18. Calculate the probability of complex events by applying the addition and multiplication rules.

Study Notes

The probability of an event is a quantitative expression of the likelihood of its occurrence. Probability is best defined in terms of relative frequency. Thus, the probability (Pr) of an event A is given by

$$Pr\,(A) = \frac{\text{number of times A does occur}}{\text{total number of times A can occur}}$$

Example: In the food poisoning epidemic described in Chapter 1, there were 99 cases of illness among the 158 people who attended the banquet. The probability of illness for a person selected at random is therefore

$$Pr\,(\text{illness}) = \frac{99}{158} = 0.63 \text{ or } 63\%$$

Notice that probabilities may be expressed as fractions, decimal fractions, or percentages. Notice also that probabilities, when expressed as decimal fractions, must fall in the range 0 to 1, so that

$$Pr\,(\text{event A does not occur}) = 1 - Pr\,(\text{event A occurs})$$

Conditional Probability

In the food poisoning example, the probability that a given person became ill was 0.63. However, the probability of illness would have to be modified if we knew what food the person ate. This introduces the idea of conditional probability or, in other words, the probability that A occurs given that B has occurred. The conditional probability for A given B is defined as

$$Pr\,(A/B) = \frac{\text{number of times A and B occur jointly}}{\text{number of times B occurs}}$$

Example: Suppose we want to determine the probability of illness for people who ate turkey at the banquet. Expressed as a conditional probability this is

$$Pr\,(\text{illness/ate turkey}) = \frac{\text{number who ate turkey and became ill}}{\text{number who ate turkey}}$$

$$= \frac{97}{133} = 0.73 \text{ or } 73\%$$

If the events A and B are independent, that is, if the occurrence of one does not influence the occurrence of the other, then

$$Pr\,(A/B) = Pr\,(A)$$

Complex Events

Events expressed as specified combinations (e.g., A and B) and events expressed as specified alternatives (e.g., A or B) are called complex events.

Pr (A and B) = probability that A and B occur jointly.

If A and B cannot occur jointly, they are called *mutually exclusive* and Pr (A and B) = 0.

Pr (A or B) = probability that A occurs or B occurs or both occur.

In other words, Pr (A or B) expresses the probability that at least one of the stated alternatives occurs.

There are two rules for combining probabilities that will enable us to deal with complex events more easily. These are the multiplication rule and the addition rule.

The Multiplication Rule

The multiplication rule states that

$$Pr\,(A \text{ and } B) = Pr\,(A/B)\,Pr\,(B)$$

So that when A and B are independent, we have

$$Pr (A \text{ and } B) = Pr (A) Pr (B)$$

Example: Side effects with a certain drug occur in 10% of all patients who take it. A physician has two patients who are taking the drug. What is the probability that both experience side effects?

Here we can assume that the events in question are independent, that is, the occurrence of side effects in one patient does not affect the likelihood of side effects in the other patient. Then,

$$Pr (\text{both experience side effects}) = 0.1 \times 0.1 = 0.01 \text{ or } 1\%$$

The Addition Rule

The addition rule states that

$$Pr (A \text{ or } B) = Pr (A) + Pr (B) - Pr (A \text{ and } B)$$

and when A and B are mutually exclusive,

$$Pr (A \text{ or } B) = Pr (A) + Pr (B)$$

Example: What is the probability that at least one of the physician's patients experiences side effects?
Notice that the events are not mutually exclusive, and, therefore,

$$Pr (\text{at least one experiences side effects}) = 0.1 + 0.1 - 0.01$$
$$= 0.19 \text{ or } 19\%$$

Exercises

Serum Uric Acid Levels in Healthy Males

The frequency distribution of serum uric acid for 267 healthy male adults is given in Table 5–1 (p. 48). Use this table to answer the following:

1. **What is the probability that a healthy male will have a serum uric acid level in the range of 4.0 to 5.9 mg/dl?**
2. **That he will have a level below 4.0 mg/dl?**
3. **That he will have a level below 4.0 or above 5.9 mg/dl?**

Organ Damage in Hypertensive Patients

A study of end organ damage (Entwisle et al., 1977) was done on hypertensive patients seen at the University of Maryland Hypertension Clinic. Table 6–1 was compiled from 306 newly identified cases of hypertension and shows evidence of end organ damage classified by severity of hypertension.

4. What is the probability that a new patient with hypertension coming to the clinic will have a history of angina?
5. Given that the patient has severe hypertension, what is the probability for a history of angina?
6. What is the probability that a new patient coming to the clinic will have a normal electrocardiogram?
7. Given that the new patient with hypertension has a normal electrocardiogram, what is the probability that the hypertension is severe?
8. What is the probability that a new patient coming to the clinic will have a history of angina and a normal electrocardiogram?
9. What is the probability that a new patient coming to the clinic will have a history of angina or an abnormal electrocardiogram?
10. Two new patients with hypertension come to the clinic on the same day. What is the probability that both have abnormal electrocardiograms?
11. What is the probability that at least one of the two new patients has a history of angina?

Table 6–1 End Organ Damage in Hypertension Patients

		Severity of Hypertension		
		Mild to Moderate	Severe	All
History of angina	+	18	7	25
	−	243	38	281
	all	261	45	306
History of stroke	+	4	1	5
	−	257	44	301
	all	261	45	306
Electrocardiographic abnormality	+	56	22	78
	−	205	23	228
	all	261	45	306

Exercise Answers

1. 0.652 or 65.2%.
2. 0.064 or 6.4%.
3. 0.349 or 34.9%.

   Notice that this probability may be determined by using the addition rule:

   Pr (below 4.0) + Pr (above 5.9)

   since the two "events" are mutually exclusive, or alternatively, by

   1 – Pr (between 4.0 and 5.9)

4. 25/306 = 0.082 or 8.2%.
5. 7/45 = 0.156 or 15.6%.
6. 228/306 = 0.745 or 74.5%.
7. 23/228 = 0.101 or 10.1%.
8. We cannot determine this because the "events" are not independent, and therefore

   Pr (angina and normal electrocardiogram) ≠ Pr (angina) × Pr (normal electrocardiogram)

   Notice that if we could get

   Pr (angina/normal electrocardiogram),

   we could compute the probability needed for the answer. However, this is not possible with the data as provided.

9. It is again impossible to answer this. Since the events are not mutually exclusive, we must use

   Pr (angina or abnormal electrocardiogram) =

   Pr (angina) + Pr (abnormal electrocardiogram)

   – Pr (angina and abnormal electrocardiogram)

   We cannot obtain the last term in this expression for the same reasons we could not answer question 8.

10. In this case the events are independent, and thus the answer is

$$\frac{78}{306} \times \frac{78}{306} = 0.065 \text{ or } 6.5\%.$$

11. $0.082 + 0.082 - (0.082)^2 = 0.157$ or 15.7%.

Reference

Entwisle, G., Apostolides, A.Y., Hebel, J.R., and Henderson, M.M. 1977. Target damage in black hypertensives. Circulation 55:792.

Recommended Readings

Elston, R.C., and Johnson, W.D. *Essentials of Biostatistics.* Philadelphia, F.A. Davis Co., 1994. Chapter 4 provides the basic concepts of probability, with examples taken mainly from genetics.

Ingelfinger, J.A., Mosteller, F., Thibodeau, L.A., and Ware, J.H. *Biostatistics in Clinical Medicine.* New York, McGraw-Hill Inc., 1994. In Chapter 1, probability is introduced in the context of diagnostic testing.

7

Screening

Objectives Covered

19. Define *sensitivity, specificity,* and *predictive value* of a screening test, and compute these measures given the necessary data.
20. Describe the selection of screening test criteria with respect to the natural history of the disease in question.

Study Notes

Screening

A screening test is used to separate from a large group of *apparently well* persons those who have a high probability of having the disease under study, so that they may be given a diagnostic workup and, if diseased, can be treated.

In general, screening is performed only when the following conditions are met:

1. The target disease is an important cause of mortality and morbidity.
2. A proven and acceptable test exists to detect individuals at an early stage of disease.
3. There is treatment available to prevent mortality and morbidity once positives have been identified.

Sensitivity and Specificity

There are two probabilities used to measure the ability of a screening test to discriminate between individuals who have the disease and those who do not. These components are determined by comparing the results obtained by the screening test with those derived from some definitive diagnostic procedure. The extent to which the screening results agree with those derived by the more definitive tests provides a measure of sensitivity and specificity.

Sensitivity is the ability of the screening test to give a positive finding when the person tested truly has the disease. It is expressed as a percentage:

$$\frac{\text{people with the disease detected by screening test}}{\text{total number of people tested with the disease}} \times 100$$

It may seem that sensitivity alone is all one would demand of a test. If it can correctly identify all those with the disease, surely that is sufficient. However, it is necessary that it include as positives only those individuals with the disease. From this constraint stems the concept of specificity.

Specificity is the ability of the test to give a negative finding when the subjects tested are free of the disease under study. It is also expressed as a percentage:

$$\frac{\text{people without the disease who are negative to the screening test}}{\text{total number of people tested without the disease}} \times 100$$

Sensitivity and specificity of a screening test can be understood more easily by using an example such as glaucoma, a disease in which intraocular pressure has increased.

The investigator has the problem of setting the cutoff point, or the reading above which a patient shall be considered by screening to have glaucoma. By studying Figure 7–1, it is apparent that to detect all glaucomatous eyes (i.e., to attain sensitivity of 100%), the cutoff must be at 22 mm Hg. This level will result in detection of all glaucoma, but at the price of including a considerable number of normal eyes, those in the right-hand tail of the nonglaucomatous distribution, from 22 to 27. This means that the specificity is less than 100%.

Now let us assume that it is desired to exclude all normal eyes, that is, to have a specificity of 100%. Clearly this entails setting the cutoff point at 27, and thus all normals will be excluded and only glaucomatous eyes detected. However, the price of this will be that some glaucoma is missed, that is, sensitivity is less than 100%.

In practice, a compromise is reached and the cutoff point is set at, for example, 24. This means that both the sensitivity and specificity are less than 100%, and both false-positive and false-negative results will arise, but in small numbers. By studying Figure 7–1, it is apparent that the sensitivity and specificity cannot both be 100%, while the distributions of well and diseased populations overlap with respect to the variable being measured by the screening test. Since the screening test result depends on one cutoff reading only, invariably sensitivity and specificity are related.

In a single test sensitivity may be increased but only at the expense of specificity, and, similarly, specificity may be increased at the expense of sensitivity. The cutoff point may be moved in the common territory shared by the well and the diseased, and a reciprocal relationship exists between sensitivity and specificity.

The actual setting depends on clinical considerations peculiar to the disease under study. Both the natural history of the disease and the effectiveness of intervention,

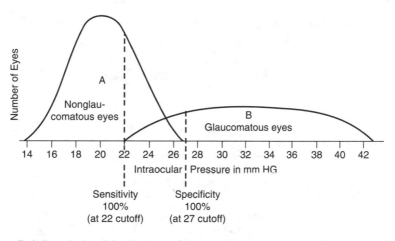

Figure 7–1 Population Distribution of Intraocular Pressures in Glaucomatous and Nonglaucomatous Eyes, Measured by Tonometer (Hypothetical Readings). *Source:* Modified from Thorner and Remein, 1961

both early and late, must be known. If the disease is very rare, sensitivity must be high, or else the few cases present will be missed (phenylketonuria is such an example). If the disease has a latent period in development, during which it is asymptomatic, yet may be detected by a screening test and prognosis improved, screening is very rewarding. If the disease is very lethal and early detection markedly improves prognosis, high sensitivity is necessary. The cancers generally are such examples, in which false-positive results are tolerable, but false-negative results are not. On the other hand, in a prevalent disease for which treatment does not markedly alter outcome, specificity must be high, otherwise the facility is overwhelmed by diagnostic demands on all the positive findings, both true and false.

Computation of Sensitivity and Specificity

From Table 7–1 it may be seen that

$$\text{sensitivity} = \frac{a}{a + c}$$

Students always get this right, *but*

$$\text{specificity} = \frac{d}{b + d}$$

This is tricky, and students sometimes make the error of using $b/(b + d)$ by false analogy from sensitivity.

In order to construct such a table from data given in narrative form, it is recommended that you fill in the marginal totals first, before the individual cells.

Table 7–1 A General Representation of a Screening Matrix

Test Result	True Diagnosis		Total
	Diseased	Not Diseased	
Positive	a	b	a + b
Negative	c	d	c + d
Total	a + c	b + d	a + b + c + d

False-Positive and False-Negative Results

The clinician thinks in terms of false-positive *(b)* and false-negative *(c)* results. A test that is very sensitive has few false-negative results—remember that sensitivity is $a/(a + c)$, so c is small when sensitivity approaches 100%.

A test with a high specificity will have few false-positive findings, since specificity is $d/(d + b)$; therefore, for specificity to approach 100%, b must be small.

Predictive Value of a Positive Test

From Table 7–1 it will be seen that the proportion of positive tests that are truly positive is $a/(a + b)$. This ratio is called the predictive value of a positive test. Physicians are responsible for interpreting for the positive screenees, the meaning of their positive result and selecting those with the true positive tests *(a)* from the group *(a + b)*. The predictive value of a positive test increases with increasing sensitivity and specificity, as might be expected. But if the prevalence of the disease in the population screened increases, the predictive value of a positive test also increases, and the converse is true. High-risk populations are frequently chosen for screening, thus increasing the yield and predictive value of a positive test.

In Table 7–2 the prevalence of disease is 50%, the sensitivity and specificity are both 50%, and the number screened is 200. From these data the predictive value of a positive test is 50/100 or 50%. In Table 7–3 the prevalence increases to 60% and the sensitivity and specificity remain at 50%. From the data shown the predictive value of a positive test has now increased to 60/100 or 60%. In Table 7–4, the prevalence decreases to 40% and the sensitivity and specificity remain at 50%. From the data shown the predictive value of a positive test has now decreased to 40/100, or 40%.

Acceptability

Acceptability of a screening test is a practical consideration. For example, a cervical smear is more acceptable than sigmoidoscopy. High-risk groups are fre-

Table 7–2

| Test Result | True Diagnosis | | Total |
	Disease	No Disease	
Positive	50	50	100
Negative	50	50	100
Total	100	100	200

Table 7–3

| Test Result | True Diagnosis | | Total |
	Disease	No Disease	
Positive	60	40	100
Negative	60	40	100
Total	120	80	200

Table 7–4

| Test Result | True Diagnosis | | Total |
	Disease	No Disease	
Positive	40	60	100
Negative	40	60	100
Total	80	120	200

quently identified as target populations for screening programs; yet acceptance is often lowest among those with the greatest probability of disease, for example, the very old or those of low educational attainment.

Exercises

Table 7–5 shows the results obtained in a screening test for diabetes used on 10,000 persons. The cutoff level was a blood glucose value of 180 mg/dl or above as positive for diabetes.

Table 7–5 Results of Screening Test for Diabetes

	True Diagnosis		
Test Result	Diabetic	Not Diabetic	Total
Positive	34	20	54
Negative	116	9,830	9,946
Total	150	9,850	10,000

1. **Compute the fractions representing sensitivity, specificity, and predictive value of a positive test.**

   When the screening cutoff point was lowered to a blood glucose value of 130 mg/dl, 98 of 164 persons who then tested positive were among the 9,850 persons judged by diagnostic tests not to have diabetes.

2. **Compute the sensitivity, specificity, and predictive value of a positive test at this cutoff level.**
3. **What effect do you get from lowering the screening cutoff point in terms of false-positive and false-negative findings and predictive value of a positive test?**
4. **How does this affect the sensitivity?**
5. **If the cutoff point is set higher than 180 mg/dl, then**
   a. **how would you expect this to affect the specificity and sensitivity of the test?**
   b. **what effect will this have on the number of false-negative and false-positive findings?**
6. **In Table 7–5 assume the prevalence of diabetes increases from 1.5% to 2.0%. Given the same sensitivity and specificity, compute the predictive value of a positive test.**
7. **Your screening facility can process 1,000 people per week. Assume you are attempting the early detection of a disease with a prevalence of 2%, and that your test has a sensitivity of 95% and a specificity of 90%.**
   a. **How many of the people screened in a week will test positive?**
   b. **Of these, in how many will the results be truly positive and in how many will they be falsely positive?**
   c. **What is the predictive value of a positive test?**
8. **Suggest a disease for each of the following in which screening leading to early diagnosis has been shown to affect the outcome favorably:**
   a. **for the individual**
   b. **for the community in general (including the nondiseased segment)**

Exercise Answers

1. Sensitivity = 34/150 or 22.6%.
   Specificity = 9830/9850 or 99.7%.
   Predictive value of a positive test = 34/54 or 63.0%.
2. The new values at cutoff of 130 mg/dl would be those shown in Table 7–6.

Table 7–6

Test Result	True Diagnosis		Total
	Diabetic	Nondiabetic	
Positive	66	98	164
Negative	84	9,752	9,836
Total	150	9,850	10,000

Sensitivity = 66/150 or 44%.

Specificity = 9752/9850 or 99%.

Predictive value of a positive test = 66/164 or 40%.

3. Lowering the screening cutoff level of blood glucose that distinguishes between diseased and nondiseased populations will increase the false-positive findings, decrease the false-negative findings, and decrease the predictive value of a positive test.
4. Sensitivity will be increased, and specificity will be decreased.
5. a. If the cutoff level is set higher than 180 mg/dl, the specificity will be increased and the sensitivity will be decreased.
   b. False-negative findings increase, and false-positive findings decrease.
6. Table 7–5 now becomes Table 7–7:

Table 7–7

Test Result	True Diagnosis		Total
	Diabetic	Nondiabetic	
Positive	45	20	65
Negative	155	9,780	9,935
Total	200	9,800	10,000

Predictive value of a positive test is $a/(a + b) = 45/65$ or **69%**. Note that the increase in prevalence from **1.5%** to **2.0%** has increased the predictive value of a positive test.

7. Out of 1,000 people screened, 20 will have the disease, a prevalence of 2%. Sensitivity of 95% means that $a/(a + c) = 95/100$. Now, $a + c = 20$, thus $a = 19, c = 1$. Specificity of 90% means that $d/(b + d) = 90/100$. Now, $b + d = 980$, thus $b = 98, d = 882$. (See Table 7–8.)

Table 7–8

Screening	Diagnosis		Total
	Positive	Negative	
Positive	19	98	117
Negative	1	882	883
Total	20	980	1,000

a. An examination of Table 7–8 indicates that 117 individuals will test positive per week.
b. Of these, 19 will be true positives and 98 will be false positives.
c. Predictive value of a positive test = 19/117 or 16.2%.

8. a. Two examples of screening that is beneficial to the individual are
   1) screening for cervical cancer, in all age groups, by cytology
   2) screening for breast cancer by mammography, which is beneficial to women older than 50 years of age
   b. Two examples of screening that is beneficial to the community are
   1) screening for streptococcal infection to prevent rheumatic fever
   2) skin testing for tuberculosis

Reference

Thorner, R.M., and Remein, Q.R. 1961. Principles and procedures in the evaluation of screening for disease. Public Health Monograph #67.

Recommended Readings

Fletcher, R.H., Fletcher, S.W., and Wagner, E.H. *Clinical Epidemiology: The Essentials.* Baltimore, Williams & Wilkins, 1988. Screening concepts within the broader context of disease prevention are presented in Chapter 8.

Galen, R.S., and Gambino, S.R. *Beyond Normality: The Predictive Value and Efficiency of Medical Diagnoses.* New York, John Wiley & Sons, 1975. This text is a very thorough and extensive discussion of the statistical aspects of disease detection.

Mausner, J.S., and Kramer, S. *Mausner and Bahn: Epidemiology—An Introductory Text.* 2d ed. Philadelphia, W.B. Saunders Co., 1985. Chapter 9 emphasizes the use of screening as a means for achieving secondary prevention.

Riegelman, R.K., and Hirsch, R.P. *Studying a Study and Testing a Test: How To Read the Medical Literature.* 2d ed. Boston, Little, Brown and Company, 1989. Part 2 is a highly readable discussion of the issues relating to screening, especially useful are the flaw-catching exercises.

8

Sampling

Objectives Covered

21. Use the standard error to compute 95% confidence limits for a mean or a proportion, and interpret statements containing confidence limits.
22. Explain sampling bias, and describe how random sampling operates to avoid bias in the process of data collection.
23. Distinguish between the standard deviation and the standard error, and give one example of the use of each.

Study Notes

The Target Population

The target population is that collection of individuals, items, measurements, etc., about which we want to make inferences. We seldom have data on the entire target population. Instead, we must rely on the information provided by a sample. To make generalizations on the basis of sample results, it is necessary to consider how the sample relates to the target population.

Sampling Error

Sampling error is the difference between the sample result and the population characteristic we seek to estimate. In practice, the sampling error can rarely be determined because the population characteristic is not usually known. However, with appropriate sampling procedures it can be kept small and the investigator can determine the probable limits of its magnitude.

There are two factors that contribute to sampling error:

1. biased selection
2. random variation

A biased selection is one from an unrepresentative segment of the population. The error that results cannot be determined. However, even if the sample were chosen in an unbiased way, we would not expect it to be a perfect replica of the population. The sampling error in this case is attributable strictly to chance, and we may think of it as arising from the random variation that would occur from sample to sample (if repeated sampling were done from the same population).

Random Sampling

If the sample is selected in a way that gives each member of the population an equal chance of being chosen, it is a random sample. There are two desirable features of a random sample:

1. It eliminates bias.
2. It enables us to determine the reliability of our result.

For a random sample the only source of sampling error is random variation. Such variation is determined by the heterogeneity of the population and by the size of the sample.

The Standard Error

Just as the variability of a measurement is characterized by the standard deviation, the variability of a sample statistic (such as a mean or a proportion) is characterized by the standard error. The smaller the standard error, the more reliable is the statistic. The primary use of the standard error is in constructing confidence intervals.

Confidence Limits

The confidence interval is a useful device for making inferences about the population parameter in which we are interested. In the case of a 95% confidence interval, we can say that there is a 95% chance that the interval will include the population parameter. For reasonably large samples, generally including 25 or more units, the 95% confidence limits can be expressed as sample statistic ± 2 standard errors.

Exercises

Cesarean Sections in Baltimore

To determine the proportion of cesarean sections among obstetrical deliveries in Baltimore, a random sample of histories was obtained from two obstetrical services: Johns Hopkins Hospital and University Hospital. The rate of cesarean sections for the sample was 20%. Later more complete information revealed that it was not indicative of the general experience throughout the city. Most hospitals in the city were found to have rates ranging from 10% to 12%.

1. **What constitutes the "target population" for this study?**
2. **Why would you regard the sample as biased, even though a random selection of histories was obtained?**

Symptoms of Heart Disease

In an attempt to document the duration between onset of symptoms of heart disease and first attack of myocardial infarction, the experience of 330 patients was recorded (Sigler, 1951). These patients had all complained of symptoms to a physician at some time prior to their attack. Their records were used to determine the time from onset of symptoms to attack. The results are given in Table 8–1.

3. **How would you define the target population for this study?**
4. **What sorts of cases would tend to be missed from the kind of sample used to measure the duration between onset of symptoms and attack? How would such omissions affect the results?**
5. **Two other methods of determining duration might be considered:**
   a. **asking patients to recall the onset of symptoms after their attacks**
   b. **following patients from the time they first report symptoms (including those who never develop an attack)**
   What approach would provide the most accurate information?
6. **What might account for the very long durations given in Table 8–1?**

Labile Hypertension

A patient who at one time is hypertensive and at another time is normotensive presents a perplexing problem (Julius et al., 1974). A study was made of men who had at least one blood pressure reading over 140 mm Hg systolic or 90 mm Hg

Table 8–1 Duration Between Onset of Symptoms of Heart Disease and First Attack of Myocardial Infarction

Duration	Number of Cases
1 day	4
2–6 days	12
1–3 weeks	20
1–2 months	28
3–6 months	54
7–11 months	45
1–2 years	50
3 years	23
4 years	22
5 years	16
6 years	12
7 years	8
8 years	12
9 years	4
10 years or more	20
Total	330

diastolic and at least one reading under 140/90 mm Hg for a series of clinic visits. Men of similar age but whose blood pressure was never found to be over 140/90 mm Hg served as a control group. In the hypertensive group, a subgroup was identified consisting of those men whose blood pressure returned to normal when taken at home. It was of particular interest to determine what characteristics of these labile hypertensives might be used to distinguish them from normotensives.

7. Determine 95% confidence limits for each measure given in Table 8–2.

Table 8–2 Clinical Characteristics (Mean or Proportion ± Standard Error) of Subjects in Different Blood Pressure Categories

Characteristic	Normal in Clinic (N = 49)	Borderline in Clinic but Normal at Home (N = 31)
Weight (kg)	70.6 ± 1.5	81.3 ± 1.9
Heart rate (beats per minute)	70.9 ± 1.4	83.1 ± 2.1
Positive family history (%)	24.4 ± 6.1	41.9 ± 8.9

8. Which characteristics would you regard as having differences too large to be attributed to "sampling error" alone? Why?

The following rule was used to establish which cases of borderline hypertension could be regarded as having normal readings at home. If the man's home reading was not higher than 1 standard deviation from the mean home reading among clinical normals (the control group) on both systolic and diastolic blood pressure, he was classified as being normal at home.

9. What is the rationale for this rule?
10. Explain the difference between the use of the standard deviation and the standard error in this problem.

Exercise Answers

1. All obstetrical cases in Baltimore.
2. The sample was restricted by the hospitals used in the study. These are the two teaching hospitals in the city and therefore would be expected to handle an unusually large proportion of difficult cases.
3. To generalize the results in order to make a statement about the duration between symptoms and first attack of myocardial infarction, it seems reasonable to define the target population as all cases of myocardial infarction with prior symptoms.
4. The main source of omission would be unreported symptoms. This could occur for a number of reasons:
   a. death during the time of the first attack
   b. failure of the patient to recognize or report symptoms
   c. faulty recall
   Omission would seem most likely to occur whenever duration was very short and the patient did not have time to inform a physician. This would lead to underreporting.
5. The second approach provides the most accurate information. We would not expect to get as accurate an account of symptoms after the attack has occurred. The patient's state of mind would no doubt influence his ability to recall symptoms as they actually happened. For those cases in which the victim died, we would have to rely on family or friends for such information.
6. The longer the duration, the more likely it is that there were errors in reporting. Such errors might arise by failure to report attacks. It would also seem probable that the longer the duration, the less the symptoms would have to do with heart disease.

7. See Table 8–3

Table 8–3 Ninety-Five Percent Confidence Limits on Characteristics of Subjects in Different Blood Pressure Categories

Characteristic	Normal in Clinic	Borderline in Clinic but Normal at Home
Mean weight (kg)	67.6–73.6	77.5–85.1
Mean heart rate (beats per minute)	68.1–73.7	78.9–87.3
Proportion with positive family history (%)	12.2–36.6	24.1–59.7

8. Those for weight and heart rate. For each of these characteristics there is no overlap in the confidence intervals for the two groups. On the other hand there is considerable overlap in the confidence intervals for family history.
9. Assuming that the distribution of blood pressure readings among those who were established as normotensive at the clinic follows the normal curve, and that this group is truly normotensive, the rule would lead to misclassifying approximately 16% of those who would be really normotensive at home as being hypertensive. (See Figure 5–4 "The Normal Distribution Curve," page 51).
10. The standard deviation expresses variability among individuals and is used therefore to make decisions about individuals. The standard error expresses variability in group statistics and is thus used to make inferences about groups.

References

Julius, S., Ellis, C.N., Pascual, A.V., Matice, M., Hansson, L., Hunzor, S.N., and Sandler, L.N. 1974. Home blood pressure determination. JAMA 229:663.

Sigler, L.H. 1951. Prognosis of angina pectoris and coronary occlusion. JAMA 146:998.

Recommended Readings

Bland, M. *An Introduction to Medical Statistics.* Oxford, Oxford Medical Publications, 1987. Chapter 8 provides a thorough description of the rationale and application of confidence intervals.

Rimm, A.A., Hartz, A.J., Kalbfleisch, J.H., Anderson, A.J., and Hoffmann, R.G. *Basic Biostatistics in Medicine and Epidemiology.* New York, Appleton-Century-Crofts, 1980. Chapter 2 discusses sampling issues in the context of a class epidemiologic study, and Chapter 11 gives a good discussion of the distinction between the standard deviation and the standard error.

9

Statistical Significance

Objectives Covered

24. Interpret statements of statistical significance with regard to comparisons of means and frequencies, and explain what is meant by a statement such as "$P < 0.05$."
25. Distinguish between the statistical significance of a result and its importance in clinical application.

Study Notes

Interpretation of Comparison Results

The term *statistically significant* is often encountered in scientific literature, and yet its meaning is still widely misunderstood. The determination of statistical significance is made by the application of a procedure called at statistical test. Such procedures are useful for interpreting comparison results. For example, suppose that a clinician finds that in a small series of patients the mean response to treatment is greater for drug A than for drug B. Obviously the clinician would like to know if the observed difference in this small series of patients will hold up for a population of such patients. In other words he wants to know whether the observed difference is more than merely "sampling error." This assessment can be made with a statistical test.

To understand better what is meant by statistical significance, let us consider the three possible reasons for the observed drug A versus drug B difference:

1. Drug A actually could be superior to drug B.

2. Some confounding factor that has not been controlled in any way, for example, age of the patients, may account for the difference. (In this case we would have a biased comparison.)
3. Random variation in response may account for the difference.

Only after reasons 2 and 3 have been ruled out as possibilities can we conclude that drug A is superior to drug B. To rule out reason 2, we have to have a study design that does not permit any extraneous factors to bias the comparison or else we must deal with the bias statistically, as for example by age-adjustment of rates. To rule out reason 3, we test for statistical significance. If the test shows that the observed difference is too large to be explained by random variation (chance) alone, we state that the difference is statistically significant and thus conclude that drug A is superior to drug B.

Significance Tests

Underlying all statistical tests is a *null hypothesis*. For tests involving the comparison of two or more groups, the null hypothesis states that there is no difference in population parameters among the groups being compared. In other words, the null hypothesis is consistent with the notion that the observed difference is simply the result of random variation in the data. To decide whether the null hypothesis is to be accepted or rejected, a test statistic is computed and compared with a *critical value* obtained from a set of statistical tables. When the test statistic exceeds the critical value, the null hypothesis is rejected and the difference is declared statistically significant.

Any decision to reject the null hypothesis carries with it a certain risk of being wrong. This risk is called the significance level of the test. If we test at the 5% significance level, we are taking a 5% chance of rejecting the null hypothesis when it is true. Naturally we want the significance level of the test to be small. The 5% significance level is very often used for statistical tests. A statement such as "The difference is statistically significant at the 5% level" means that the null hypothesis was rejected at the 5% significance level.

The *P* Value

Many times the investigator will report the lowest significance level at which the null hypothesis could be rejected. This level is called the *P* value. The *P* value therefore expresses the probability that a difference as large as that observed would occur by chance alone. If we see the statement *"P < 0.01,"* this means that the probability is very small that random variation alone accounts for the difference, and we are willing to say the result is statistically significant. On the other hand, the statement *"P > 0.10"* implies that chance alone is a viable explanation for the observed difference, and therefore the difference would be referred to as not statistically significant. Although arbitrary, the *P* value 0.05 is almost universally regarded as the cutoff level for statistical significance. It should be taken only as a guideline, however, because, with regard to statistical significance, a result with a *P* value of 0.051 is almost the same as one with a *P* value of 0.049.

Sample Size and the Interpretation of Nonsignificance

A statistically significant difference is one that cannot be accounted for by chance alone. The converse is not true; that is, a nonsignificant difference is not necessarily attributable to chance alone. In the case of a nonsignificant difference, the sample size is very important. This is because, with a small sample, the sampling error is likely to be large, and this often leads to a nonsignificant test even when the observed difference is caused by a real effect. In any given instance, however, there is no way to determine whether a nonsignificant difference derives from the small sample size or because the null hypothesis is correct. It is for this reason that a result that is not statistically significant should almost be regarded as inconclusive rather than an indication of no effect.

Sample size is an important aspect of study design. The investigator should consider how large the sample must be so that a real effect of important magnitude will not be missed because of sampling error. (Sample size determination for two-group comparisons is discussed by Bland [see Recommended Readings].)

Clinical Significance versus Statistical Significance

It is important to remember that a label of statistical significance does not necessarily mean that the difference is significant from the clinician's point of view. With large samples, very small differences that have little or no clinical importance may turn out to be statistically significant. The practical implications of any finding must be judged on other than statistical grounds.

Exercises

Proportionate Mortality Among Polyvinyl Chloride Workers

In February 1974, four fatal cases of cancer of the liver among men who worked in a polyvinyl chloride polymerization plant were reported (Monson, Peters, and Johnson, 1974). A proportionate mortality analysis of all deaths from 1947 to 1974 among workers in that plant is shown in Table 9–1.

Table 9–1 Observed and Expected Deaths in Polyvinyl Chloride Workers

Cause of Death	Observed	Expected	Obs./Exp.
All	161	161.0	1.0
All cancer	41	27.9	1.5
Digestive	13	8.3	1.6
Liver and biliary tract	8	0.7	11.0
Lung	13	7.9	1.6
Brain	5	1.2	4.2
Lymphatic and hemopoietic	5	3.4	1.5
Other cancer	5	7.1	0.7
Central nervous system/vascular	8	9.5	0.8
Circulatory	66	68.6	1.0
External	22	24.3	0.9
Suicide	10	5.3	1.9
All other cases	24	30.5	0.8

Note: Expected numbers based on age/time/cause-specific proportionate mortality ratios for U.S. white males.

To determine whether the excess of cancer deaths could be attributed to chance alone, we do a chi-square (χ^2) test. First, Table 9–1 is reduced to the form shown in Table 9–2.

Table 9–2 Reduced Version of Table 9–1

Cause of Death	Observed	Expected
Cancer	41	27.9
All other	120	133.1

Then the chi-square statistic is computed as

$$\chi^2 = \sum \frac{(\text{observed} - \text{expected})^2}{\text{expected}}$$

$$\chi^2 = \frac{(41-27.9)^2}{27.9} + \frac{(120-133.1)^2}{133.1} = 7.44$$

This chi-square value has one degree of freedom *(df)*, since only one of the expected numbers can be determined independently of the total number of deaths. To get the *P* value we now refer to a chi-square table. Table 9–3 is an abbreviated version of such a table, and from it we see that our computed value of chi-square exceeds that for *P* = 0.01 (for 1 *df*). We can thus report *P* < 0.01.

Table 9–3 Abbreviated Table of Chi-Square Corresponding to Selected Values of *P*

df	0.50	0.10	0.05	0.02	0.01
1	0.45	2.71	3.84	5.41	6.63
2	1.39	4.61	5.99	7.82	9.21
3	2.37	6.25	7.82	9.84	11.34
4	3.36	7.78	9.49	11.67	13.28

---

1. **Is the excess of cancer deaths statistically significant? Why?**
2. **The chi-square value for central nervous system vascular diseases is 0.04 (1 *df*). Use Table 9–2 to report a *P* value. What does the chi-square value tell you about the discrepancy of deaths in this category from the expected number?**
3. **What are the major difficulties with proportionate mortality analysis as a means of revealing the carcinogenic potential of polyvinyl chloride?**

Oral Contraceptives and Birth Defects

Exposure to exogenous sex steroids during pregnancy was investigated for 108 mothers of children with congenital limb-reduction defects and 108 mothers of normal controls (Janerich, Piper, and Glebatis, 1974). Unintentional use of oral contraceptives early in pregnancy was the primary source of exposure. Fifteen of the mothers of the affected children were found to have been exposed, whereas only four of the controls were exposed.

4. **Show, in the form of a 2 × 2 table, the results of this study.**
5. **The chi-square value for the comparisons of rates of exposure among cases and controls was 5.77 (1 *df*). (See references for computation of χ^2 from a 2 × 2 table.) Use Table 9–3 to find the corresponding *P* value. What is your interpretation of the finding?**

Low-Tar/Nicotine Cigarettes

Cigarette consumption was studied (Turner, Sillett, and Ball, 1974) in 10 volunteers smoking cigarettes of progressively lower tar/nicotine content during three consecutive periods of one week each. The subjects recorded on diary cards the number of cigarettes smoked daily. Approximately 30 cigarette butts were collected from each subject during each period. The mean consumption and butt length findings are given in Table 9–4.

Table 9–4 Cigarette Consumption and Butt Length (Means ± 2 Standard Errors) According to Tar/Nicotine Content

	Tar/Nicotine Content		
	Medium	Low	Very Low
Mean number of cigarettes consumed daily	25.7 ± 6.50	30.9 ± 8.30	29.2 ± 6.20
Mean butt length (mm)	8.84 ± 2.96	7.20 ± 2.82	4.54 ± 2.22

The following remarks are given in the paper:

When changing from medium to low brands, nine subjects increased their consumption and one reduced slightly, mean consumption rising from 25.7 to 30.9 ($P < 0.01$). There was no significant change in consumption from low to very low.

During the medium period the mean butt lengths were 8.84 mm, in the low 7.20 mm, and in the very low 4.54 mm. The difference between the low and very-low brands was statistically significant ($P < 0.01$).

6. **Did the subjects alter their smoking habits when changing to lower tar/ nicotine cigarettes? How? Is there evidence for the assertion that lower tar/nicotine cigarettes cause smokers to consume more tobacco?**

7. In the study the volunteers were informed of the tar/nicotine content of the cigarettes used during each period. What problems does this introduce? How could the study be done to avoid such problems?

Propranolol Treatment in Parkinson's Disease

Propranolol was compared with a placebo in 18 patients with Parkinson's disease who had been taking stable doses of levodopa for three months or more but who still had tremor (Marsden, Parker, and Rees, 1974). Each patient was given propranolol for a four-week period and a placebo for a similar period but was not aware of the identity of his treatment plan. A physician, who was also unaware of the treatment plan, scored each patient for total disability, tremor, rigidity, akinesia, posture, handwriting, and circle drawing. Results are given in Table 9–5.

Table 9–5 Effects of Propranolol (120 mg Daily) versus Placebo in 18 Patients with Parkinson's Disease on Levodopa

	Start Scores*	Placebo	Propranolol	Significance†
Total disability	27.80	25.70	27.60	N.S.
Tremor	2.67	2.86	2.19	N.S.
Rigidity	4.25	2.92	2.94	N.S.
Akinesia	6.58	6.06	6.75	N.S.
Posture	3.53	4.11	3.86	N.S.
Writing	1.58	1.56	1.28	$P < 0.02$
Circle drawing	1.81	1.94	1.36	$P < 0.02$

*A high score indicates severe disability.
†Propranolol compared with placebo. N.S., not significant.

8. What were the apparent benefits of the propranolol treatment?
9. The investigators concluded that the changes that were noted were "not of clinical value and none of these patients have been maintained on propranolol." In view of the fact that certain of the findings were statistically significant, what kinds of considerations would lead the investigators to this conclusion?

Exercise Answers

1. Yes. The P value found was less than 0.01, which implies that the probability is very small that the excess is attributable to chance alone. Re-

sults having P values of 0.05 or less are usually described as statistically significant.

2. Since χ^2 is less than that given in the table for $P = 0.50$, we report $P > 0.50$. This means that it is quite likely that the small difference between the expected number of deaths and the number observed is due to chance alone.

3. There are two primary problems:

   a. Proportionate mortality analysis does not take into account the absolute risk of dying in the population studied. Thus, it is possible that the mortality rate in polyvinyl chloride workers is less than that of the United States population, even though there was a disproportionate number of cancer deaths in that group.

   b. A high ratio of observed to expected deaths may be due either to an excess of one cause of death *or to a deficit of another cause.*

4. See Table 9–6

Table 9–6 Rates of Exposure to Exogenous Sex Steroids during Gestation in Children with and without Congenital Limb-Reduction Defects

	Exposed	Not Exposed	Total
Cases	15	93	108
Controls	4	104	108
Total	19	197	216

5. $P < 0.02$.

   The disparity in rates of exposures among cases and controls is too large to attribute to chance alone. Note, however, that this finding does not establish that oral contraceptives cause birth defects but only that an association exists. (See Chapter 16.)

6. The results indicate that more tobacco was consumed as the subjects moved to lower tar/nicotine content cigarettes. This is reflected by the fact that the mean number smoked was significantly higher for low as compared with medium. And although the number smoked was about the same for low and very low, the butt length comparison indicates that the subjects smoked more of each cigarette in the case of the very low tar/nicotine content type.

7. The subjects' awareness of the kind of cigarette they were smoking in each period could have influenced their consumption habits. If, for example, they had preconceived notions about the amount of satisfaction they could derive from low tar/nicotine content cigarettes, this might

have altered the number of cigarettes and the amount of each cigarette that they smoked during the various periods. The study design could have been improved by keeping the subjects "blind" to the tar/nicotine content and by randomizing the order of the three types for each subject.

8. The propranolol improved the patients' performance on the writing and circle-drawing tests. Of the several scores used to assess improvement, only these two showed statistically significant differences for the propranolol-placebo comparison.

9. Even though the drug has produced changes that cannot be attributed to chance, the clinicians had to consider what sort of changes had been produced and how large these changes were. It would seem that the clinicians, in this case, decided that neither the kind of improvement nor its extent warranted continued use of the drug.

References

Janerich, D.T., Piper, J.M., and Glebatis, D.M. 1974. Oral contraceptives and congenital limb-reduction defects. N. Engl. J. Med. 291:697.

Marsden, D.C., Parker, J.D., and Rees, J.E. 1974. Propranolol in Parkinson's Disease. Letter to the editor. Lancet 2:410.

Monson, R.R., Peters, J.M., and Johnson, M.N. 1974. Proportional mortality among vinylchloride workers. Lancet 2:397.

Turner, J.A.M., Sillett, R.W., and Ball, K.P. 1974. Some effects of changing to low-tar and low-nicotine cigarettes. Lancet 2:737.

Recommended Readings

Bland, M. *An Introduction to Medical Statistics*. Oxford, Oxford Medical Publications, 1987. Chapter 9 gives a good introduction to the principles of significance tests.

Ingelfinger, J.A., Mosteller, R., Thibodeau, L.A., and Ware, J.H. *Biostatistics in Clinical Medicine*. New York, McGraw-Hill Inc., 1994. Chapter 7 emphasizes the interpretation of P values with many clinical examples.

10

Correlation

Objectives Covered

26. Interpret the relationship between two variables as displayed on a scattergram, distinguishing between positive, negative, and zero correlation.
27. Explain the information provided by a regression equation as well as that provided by a correlation coefficient.
28. Interpret statements of statistical significance with regard to the correlation coefficient.

Study Notes

Describing Quantitative Relationships

Scientific studies often require a description of the relationship between two variables. Usually in such circumstances we think of one variable as being influenced by the other. It has become conventional to represent the dependent variable, that is, the one being influenced, as y and the independent variable as x. We are interested in describing the association between x and y. To do this we have to measure both x and y on a series of subjects.

The simplest way of describing the relationship between x and y is by a graph called a scattergram (Figure 10–1). To construct a scattergram, the level of y is plotted against the level of x for each subject. The resulting scattering of points indicates how y varies with differing levels of x.

Although the scattergram is very useful for gaining a visual impression of the relationship, a more quantitative description is often needed. Two kinds of statistical techniques are used to define the relationship between x and y:

1. regression
2. correlation

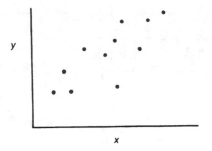

Figure 10–1 A Scattergram

The Regression Equation

The regression approach is appropriate when our main purpose is to develop a predictive model, a device that will enable us to predict y given a specified level of x.

Consider the following example. Angiotensin is a substance that raises blood pressure. Suppose we are interested in predicting changes in blood pressure when angiotensin is infused at different rates. We measure the increase in blood pressure at four different infusion rates, and we repeat our measurement four times at each infusion rate. The resulting data are plotted in Figure 10–2.

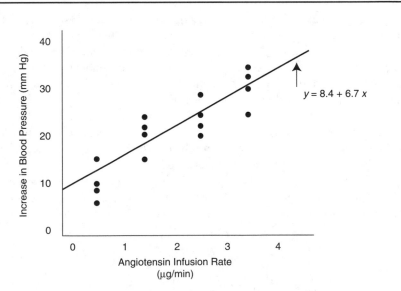

$y = 8.4 + 6.7\,x$

Figure 10–2 An Example of a Regression Line Fitted to a Set of Points

The line fitted to the points in Figure 10–2 gives us a way to predict the expected blood pressure increase at any infusion rate within the range of the graph. This line is found by a procedure called least squares, and it provides the best fit in the sense that the sum of the squared deviations of the points from the line is a minimum. The equation of the line is called the regression equation. The regression equation has the form $y = a + bx$, where a = the intercept, the value of y when x is zero, and b = the slope, the change in y resulting from a change in x of one unit. The constants a and b are found by the least squares procedure. Of the two, the slope is usually more informative because it shows how much and in which direction y will vary with changes in x.

By inserting a value for x in the regression equation we can now predict a value for y. In the example shown in Figure 10–2, we see there is some variability in the increase in blood pressure at a given infusion rate. We should therefore not expect the regression equation to predict the blood pressure increase exactly. Rather it must be thought of as providing a way of obtaining the average increase in blood pressure for a specified infusion rate.

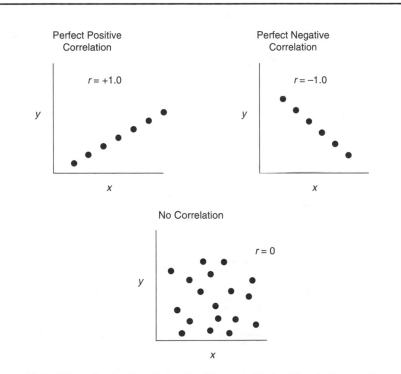

Figure 10–3 Values for the Correlation Coefficient in Perfect Correlation and No Correlation

Table 10–1 Guide to Correlation Coefficient Values

Absolute Value of r	Degree of Association
0.8–1.0	Strong
0.5–0.8	Moderate
0.2–0.5	Weak
0–0.2	Negligible

The Correlation Coefficient

The correlation coefficient, usually denoted by *r,* is an index of the extent to which two variables are associated. It can take on values between +1.0 and –1.0, depending on the strength of the association and whether a positive change in *x* produces a positive or negative change in *y.* A correlation coefficient of zero indicates the two variables are not related (Figure 10–3).

Table 10–1 can serve as a general guide to interpreting the magnitude of the correlation coefficient.

Figure 10–4 shows the correlation between survival time and liver size for 23 children with acute leukemia. In this case there is a moderate degree of associa-

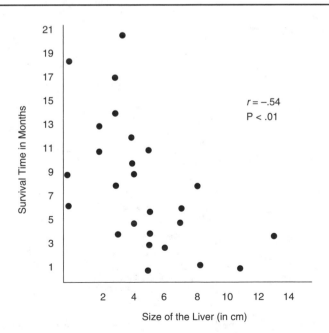

Figure 10–4 An Example of a Statistically Significant Correlation. *Source:* Modified from Halikowski, Armata, and Garwicz, 1966

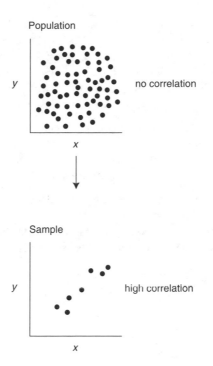

Figure 10–5 Population Correlation versus Sample Correlation

tion. Notice that the negative correlation coefficient indicates that short survival is associated with large liver size.

As with any statistic, the correlation coefficient is susceptible to sampling error. Thus, our sample may lead us to believe that there is a correlation when none actually exists in the population (Figure 10–5).

To rule out the possibility that the correlation we observe is due to chance alone, the hypothesis of no correlation can be tested statistically. The *P* value in this case is the probability that a correlation coefficient as large or larger than that observed will occur for the sample when no correlation exists in the population. In the example shown in Figure 10–4, the correlation coefficient is statistically significant at the 1% level (i.e., $P < 0.01$). We may therefore consider the probability to be very slight that the association seen between liver size and survival time is due to chance alone.

Exercises

Hemolytic Disease in Newborns

Studies have challenged the view that newborns with Coombs' test–positive hemolytic disease have abnormally high blood volumes (Brans et al., 1974). In this study the investigators attempt to show that when the hematocrit is taken into account, the blood volumes of infants with Coombs' test–positive hemolytic disease are not exceptionally high. Hematocrit, plasma volume, and blood volume were determined for 32 newborns with the disease. The observed relationship of plasma volume and blood volume to hematocrit was described in terms of the following regression equations and correlation coefficients:

$$\text{Plasma volume} = 70.3 - 0.39 \times \text{hematocrit}$$
$$r = -0.538, P < 0.005$$
$$\text{blood volume} = 60.8 + 0.79 \times \text{hematocrit}$$
$$r = 0.616, P < 0.001$$

1. **Describe the nature of the association in each case.**
2. **What do the P values indicate?**
3. **Figure 10–6 shows the blood volumes of the infants with hemolytic disease according to their hematocrit. Also shown is the regression of blood**

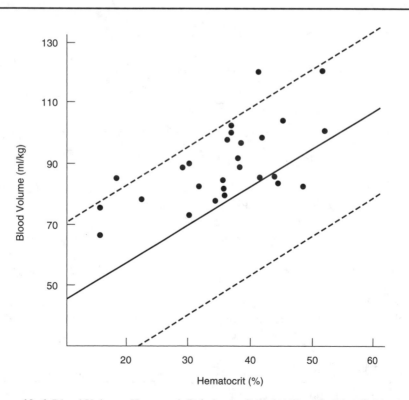

Figure 10–6 Blood Volume–Hematocrit Relation in Coombs' Test–Positive Newborns Superimposed on the Normal Range (Regression Line ±1 Standard Deviation for Normal Newborns)

volume on hematocrit for normal infants, along with the ± 1 standard deviation range. How do the infants with hemolytic disease compare with normal infants with regard to blood volume?

Colon Cancer and Blood Cholesterol

A positive correlation has been observed in international data between mortality rates for colon cancer and coronary heart disease (Rose et al., 1974). This relationship is shown in Figure 10–7.

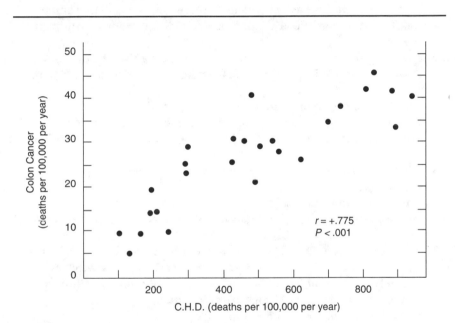

Figure 10–7 National Mortality Rates for Coronary Heart Disease (WHO List, 8th Revision, A.83) and Malignant Growths of the Intestine, Excluding Rectum (WHO List, 8th Revision, A.48), 1969 (Excluding Countries Where Either Rate Was Based on Fewer Than 50 Deaths)

4. What does this sort of association between two apparently unrelated diseases imply?
5. Is it likely that the observed correlation is simply due to chance? Why or why not?
6. Strong positive correlations have also been observed in international data between coronary heart disease and blood cholesterol level. What does this suggest concerning cholesterol and colon cancer?

7. A review of screening tests done in 90 people who subsequently died of colon cancer revealed that the majority had lower cholesterol levels than expected for their age and sex. What sort of association does this finding indicate between cholesterol and colon cancer?

Exercise Answers

1. There is a negative association between hematocrit and blood plasma, that is, high plasma volumes tend to be found in newborns with low hematocrits. A positive association exists between blood volume and hematocrit; that is, high blood volumes are found in newborns with high hematocrits.
2. In both cases the P value is very small, indicating that the probability is small that correlations of the reported magnitude would occur by chance alone.
3. Figure 10–6 shows that although newborns with this hemolytic disease tend to have higher blood volumes than the average for normal newborns, when hematocrit is taken into account, almost all fall within normal limits.
4. An association of this sort suggests shared etiological factors (common risk factors).
5. The small P value indicates that this is extremely unlikely.
6. This would suggest a positive association between serum cholesterol level and colon cancer mortality.
7. A negative association. The contradiction we have here in impressions gained from correlations made from international data with those obtained from the study of individuals indicate either of the following:
   a. Certain of these associations are artifactual.
   b. The nature of causality is complex.

References

Brans, Y.W., Milstead, R.R., Bailey, P.E., and Cassady, G. 1974. Blood volume estimates in Coombs'-test-positive infants. N. Engl. J. Med. 290:1450.

Halikowski, K., Armata, J., and Garwicz, S. 1966. Low-protein purine-free diet in treatment of acute leukemia in children: Preliminary communication. Br. Med. J. 1:519.

Rose, G., Blackburn, H., Keys, A., Taylor, H.L., Karmel, W.B., Oglesby, P., Reid, D.D., and Stamler, J. 1974. Colon cancer and blood-cholesterol. Lancet 1:181.

Recommended Readings

Bland, M. *An Introduction to Medical Statistics.* Oxford, Oxford Medical Publications, 1987. Chapter 11 is a very comprehensible description of the least squares method.

Ingelfinger, J.A., Mosteller, F., Thibodeau, L.A., and Ware, J.H. *Biostatistics in Clinical Medicine.* New York, McGraw-Hill Inc., 1994. Chapters 9 and 9A cover a wide spectrum of issues related to regression and correlation in the context of clinical problems.

11
Multiple Regression

Objectives Covered

29. Distinguish between a simple regression equation and a multiple regression equation.
30. Interpret the slope coefficients in a multiple regression as well as statements regarding their statistical significance.
31. Explain the information provided by the coefficient of determination.
32. Describe applications of the logistic and Cox proportional hazards regression models.

Study Notes

The Multiple Regression Equation

The regression equation described in Chapter 10 predicts the average value of the dependent variable y from information on a single independent variable x. When there are other variables that are predictive of y, they can be included on the right hand side of the equation as additional independent variables. If, for example, there were three independent variables the regression equation would be

$$y = a + b_1x_1 + b_2x_2 + b_3x_3$$

This is referred to as a multiple regression equation as opposed to a simple regression equation having only one independent variable. Theoretically, given enough observations a multiple regression equation can have any number of independent variables. The intercept and slope constants are obtained by a least squares procedure, which requires observations on the dependent variable and all the independent variables for each individual.

A study of the growth and development of 666 children obtained the following equation:

$$y = 21.1 + 0.0380\,x_1 + 0.00227\,x_2$$

where y is the child's weight in pounds at three years of age, x_1 is the mother's weight in pounds just prior to being pregnant with the child, and x_2 is the child's birth weight in grams. Thus for a child who weighed 3000 grams at birth and whose mother weighed 120 pounds prior to her pregnancy, the predicted weight at three years of age is 32.5 pounds.

Interpretation of the Slope Coefficients

Very often the motivation for regression analysis is not the need for a predictive model but rather the need to assess the effects of the independent variables on the dependent variable. The slope coefficients are indicators of these effects, and in multiple regression they give the effect for each variable when all the other variables on the right side of the equation are controlled (held constant). This enables the isolation of the effect of a particular variable, freed of any confounding (mediating) effects of the other independent variables.

Suppose, for example, it was desired to measure the effect of the mother's prepregnancy weight on the weight of her child at three years of age. A simple regression equation, obtained from the 666 children mentioned previously, relating weight at age three to maternal prepregnancy weight, has a slope coefficient of 0.0459. The interpretation is that for each additional pound in prepregnancy weight there is the expectation of 0.0459 additional pound in the child's weight at three years. In proposing a causal mechanism for the effect of prepregnancy weight, one might wonder whether the effect is explained by larger women having larger infants who, consequently, will be larger at three years of age, or whether there is an effect on the growth of the child subsequent to birth. To investigate the latter possibility, the birth weight must be controlled. This is accomplished by including birth weight on the right side of the regression equation. When the resulting multiple regression equation is fit to the data on the 666 children, the slope coefficient for prepregnancy weight is 0.0380. Thus, for children having the same birth weight, each additional pound in prepregnancy weight predicts an additional 0.0380 pound in the child's weight at age three. Notice that there is a reduction in the effect of prepregnancy weight after birth weight is taken into account, but some effect still remains.

Statistical significance is another important issue in the interpretation of the regression slope coefficients. In the example we have seen that there is an effect of prepregnancy weight on the child's weight at age three, even after birth weight is controlled. But can it be attributed to anything other than chance? To answer this question a statistical test is done to determine whether the slope coefficient is significantly different from zero. Tests on the two slope coefficients for the example yielded P values less than 0.001 in each case. Hence we can conclude that the effect of prepregnancy weight on the child's weight at age three is not attributable to mediation through birth weight nor is it attributable to chance alone.

It should now be recognized that multiple regression analysis provides still another method for dealing with confounding factors, whose effects must be removed before we can isolate the effect of the factor of primary interest. Other methods include the adjustment technique described in Chapter 2 and the cross-classification approach described in Chapter 16.

The Coefficient of Determination

Regarding the variation that exists in the weights of three-year-old children, there are many variables that could account for the child-to-child differences. A certain amount of the weight variation can be associated with any given variable. When a variable accounts for a large amount of the variation in another variable, the association between the two variables is strong. Since the correlation coefficient, r, indicates the strength of the association between two variables it also indicates the extent to which one variable accounts for the variation in the other. In fact, r^2 is the proportion of the variation in one that is accounted for by the other and is referred to as the coefficient of determination. For example, the correlation coefficient for prepregnancy weight and the child's weight at three years is 0.268. Thus the coefficient of determination is $(0.268)^2 = 0.072$, and we can say that 7.2% of the variation in the child's weight at age three is accounted for by the mother's prepregnancy weight. The coefficient of determination for birth weight and the child's weight at three is 0.092, indicating that birth weight accounts for slightly more of the variation in the age three weight than does the mother's prepregnancy weight.

Multiple regression analysis extends variation accounting to combinations of predictor variables via the multiple coefficient of determination R^2. This statistic indicates what proportion of variation in the dependent variable is accounted for by all the variables in the right side of the equation. The R^2 for the multiple regression equation in the example above is 0.141. This means that the mother's prepregnancy weight and the birth weight jointly account for 14.1% of the variation in the age three weight. Notice that R^2 is not simply the sum of the r^2 for prepregnancy weight and the r^2 for birth weight. That would only occur if the variables were independent of each other. Since this is not the case, then there is a degree of redundancy in the information they carry, and thus some overlap in the variation they each account for in the dependent variable.

R^2 gives an indication of how useful the multiple regression equation will be as a predictive model. If $R^2 = 1$, then the equation would predict the dependent variable for every individual without error. The variables in the right side of the equation would account for 100% of the variation. Errors in prediction could only arise if there was variation not due to variables in the model. In the example, only about 14% of the variation is accounted for by variables in the right side and 86% is left unaccounted for by these variables. The result is that the equation will not be very useful for purposes of prediction.

Other Regression Models

The regression models discussed thus far are fit by the least squares procedure, which requires that the dependent variable be a quantitative measure (e.g., weight, blood pressure). When the dependent variable is categorical (e.g., infected/not infected, normal/abnormal), another kind of regression model is used. Very often, logistic regression is used for such applications. A logistic regression equation can be used to obtain the probability that an individual falls into a given outcome category. Most often, however, interest focuses primarily on the slope coefficients. The slope coefficients in a logistic regression can be transformed into odds ratios, which for rare outcomes approximate the relative risk of the outcome for various levels of the independent variables. Moreover, odds ratios so obtained are adjusted for all the other independent variables in the regression model. Because of this capacity to derive approximate relative risks that take other factors into account, logistic regression has become a powerful analytical tool for epidemiological data.

The Cox proportional hazards model is another regression model with specialized application. While its primary application is for the analysis of survival data, the Cox model can be applied in any instance in which the dependent variable is the time to some end point (e.g., survival time, duration of hospitalization). Its most important application is when there are censored observations on the dependent variable, that is, when not all of the study subjects have reached the end point at the conclusion of the study. Since ordinary least squares regression is not possible with censored outcomes, the Cox model provides a method for getting a predictive equation. Cox regression will be discussed further in Chapter 15.

The details of the procedures used to fit the models mentioned in this chapter go beyond the scope of our book, and the reader is directed to the recommended readings if more information is needed. While the methods described in the rest of the book can usually be implemented with hand calculations, multiple regression analysis is rarely attempted without the assistance of high-speed computing equipment. This is especially true for logistic and Cox regression analyses and explains the fact that these methods were not widely applied until the necessary computing hardware and software became more available.

Exercises

A multiple regression model relating six independent variables to weight at age three was fitted to the data on 666 children mentioned previously in this chapter. The results shown in Table 11–1 were obtained.

Table 11–1 Six Independent Variables Related to Weight of Children Aged Three

Independent Variable	Slope Coefficient	P Value
Mother's height (in)	0.182	<0.01
Mother's prepregnancy weight (lb)	0.0299	<0.001
Birth weight (g)	0.00223	<0.001
Gestation (wk)	−0.222	<0.01
Length at birth (cm)	0.0631	>0.10
Head circumference at birth (cm)	0.0418	>0.10

Intercept = 14.8
$R^2 = 0.167$

1. **What weight is predicted for a child who was born after 39 weeks' gestation and who, at birth, weighed 2800 g, was 50 cm long, had a 34-cm head circumference and whose mother was 62 inches tall and weighed 100 pounds prior to pregnancy?**
2. **Describe the quantitative effect of gestation on the child's weight at age three when the other five independent variables are taken into account. Is this effect likely to be the result of chance alone?**
3. **Do #2 for the effect of birth length.**
4. **How much additional variation in weight at age three is accounted for by the four new variables in the model?**

   For the objectives listed below indicate which of the following models would provide the most appropriate regression equation:
   a. least squares
   b. logistic
   c. Cox proportional hazards

_____5. **to determine the effect of age on the time to recover from fracture of the hip.**
_____6. **to estimate the effect of packs of cigarettes smoked during pregnancy on the birth weight while controlling for the mother's age, parity, and prepregnancy weight.**

_____7. to estimate the risk of death during a hospital stay associated with previous history of heart disease while controlling for age, sex, and socioeconomic status.

Exercise Answers

1. $14.8 + (0.182)(62) + (0.0299)(100) + (0.00223)(2800) + (-0.222)(39) + (0.0631)(50) + (0.0418)(34) = 31.2$ pounds
2. With all other independent variables held constant, an increment of one week's gestation results in a reduction of 0.222 pound in the expected value of the child's weight at age three. Due to the small P value attached to the slope coefficient ($P < 0.01$), this effect is not likely to be attributable to chance alone.
3. With all other independent variables held constant, an additional centimeter of birth length is expected to result in an increase of 0.0631 pound for weight at age three. This effect may be due to chance alone, however, because the slope coefficient is not statistically significant ($P > 0.10$).
4. From the information given in the Study Notes, we see that prepregnancy weight and birth weight account for 14.1% of the variation in age three weight. $R^2 = 0.167$ for the model that includes four new independent variables. Thus the new variables only account for an additional 2.6% of the variation in weight at three.
5. c. Cox proportional hazards. This is the model of choice because the dependent variable is time to an end point (i.e., recovery from the hip fracture). Note also that there will probably be censored observations due to patients who die before they recover.
6. a. Least squares. Since birth weight is a quantitative measure, a conventional least squares approach can be used to obtain a model with birth weight as the dependent variable and packs of cigarettes during pregnancy, age, parity, and prepregnancy weight as the independent variables.
7. b. Logistic. Here there is a categorical dependent variable (i.e., surviving the hospital stay or not). The independent variables would be previous history of heart disease, age, parity, and socioeconomic status. The slope coefficient for history of heart disease can be used to obtain the odds ratio on death for those with such history relative to those without, adjusted for age, sex, and socioeconomic status.

Recommended Readings

Kahn, H.A., and Sempos, C.T. *Statistical Methods in Epidemiology*. New York, Oxford University Press, 1989. Chapters 6 and 7 emphasize regression analysis of epidemiological data, especially for the purpose of adjustment.

Kleinbaum, D.G., Kupper, L.L., and Muller, K.E. *Applied Regression Analysis and Other Multivariable Methods*. 2d ed. Boston, PWS-Kent, 1988. Chapters 8 through 16 provide a comprehensive treatment of all aspects of least squares regression analysis, including computational procedures.

Mathews, D.E., and Farewell, V. *Using and Understanding Medical Statistics*. New York, Karger, 1985. Chapters 10 through 12 focus mainly on interpretation of the results of regression analyses and include examples of least squares, logistic, and Cox proportional hazards models.

Self-Assessment 2

Objectives Covered: 12–32

Best Choice—Select *One* Answer Only

A hypertension screening program was carried out in an urban population. Results for diastolic blood pressure among 1,500 males, aged 30 to 69, are shown in Table A2–1.

Table A2–1 Frequency of Diastolic Blood Pressure in Urban Men Aged 30 to 69

Diastolic Blood Pressure (mm Hg)	Frequency	Percent
<65	60	4
65–74	270	18
75–84	540	36
85–94	420	28
95–104	150	10
105–115	45	3
>115	15	1
Total	1500	100

Use these data for questions 26 through 29.

26. Diastolic blood pressure levels of 95 or over were considered to be hypertensive and such cases were referred for further diagnosis. Thus, further testing was initiated for men whose results
   a. fell above the 86th percentile
   b. fell above the 97.5th percentile
   c. fell above the 95th percentile
   d. fell below the 14th percentile
   e. fell below the 28th percentile
27. Assuming that the men screened were representative of all men aged 30 to 69 in this urban population, the probability that a man selected at random will have a diastolic blood pressure of 105 mm Hg or higher is
   a. 3%
   b. 4%
   c. 14%
   d. 86%
   e. 96%

28. Both the mean and median of the blood pressure distribution are approximately 83 mm Hg, and the standard deviation is 12 mm Hg. These indices enable us to deduce each of the following statements *except*
    a. Approximately 95% of the men have diastolic blood pressure between 59 and 107 mm Hg.
    b. The distribution is nearly symmetrical.
    c. The 95% confidence limits on the mean for all men, aged 30 to 69, in this population are 59 and 107 mm Hg.
    d. Approximately half of the men have diastolic blood pressures over 83 mm Hg.
    e. The mean is not distorted very much by extremely high pressures in this case.
29. The distribution of diastolic blood pressure for 800 females in this population is nearly symmetrical, with about the same standard deviation as that for the males. The mean for the females was 79 mm Hg. Thus we may conclude the following:
    a. The median will be the same as that for the males.
    b. The normal range will be the same as that for the males.
    c. The standard error of the mean will be the same as that for the males.
    d. There will be a larger proportion of hypertensive females than males.
    e. There will be a smaller proportion of hypertensive females than males.
30. A correlation between two variables measures the degree to which they are
    a. mutually exclusive
    b. causally related
    c. associated
    d. statistically significant
    e. positively skewed
31. The mean birth weight of first-born infants of 23 women who smoked more than one pack of cigarettes per day during pregnancy was 200 g lower than that of the first-born infants of 16 women who never smoked. The difference was statistically significant at the 5% level ($P < 0.05$). This means which of the following?
    a. Smoking during pregnancy retards fetal growth.
    b. The difference observed between mean birth weights was too large to have occurred by chance alone.
    c. The difference observed between mean birth weights could have easily occurred by chance alone.
    d. The number of patients studied was not sufficient to achieve a conclusive result.
    e. Smoking during pregnancy does not influence fetal growth.

A screening test for breast cancer was administered to 400 women with biopsy-proven breast cancer and to 400 women without breast cancer. The test results were positive for 100 of the proven cases and 50 of the normal women. Use these data for questions 32, 33, and 34.

32. The sensitivity of the test is
    a. 88%
    b. 67%
    c. 25%
    d. 33%
    e. 12%
33. The specificity of the test is
    a. 88%
    b. 67%
    c. 25%
    d. 33%
    e. 12%
34. The predictive value of a positive test is
    a. 88%
    b. 67%
    c. 25%
    d. 33%
    e. 12%
35. Five percent of pregnant women have evidence of urinary tract infection when they are first seen for prenatal care. Four percent of those who are not found to be infected at the first prenatal visit develop an infection between that time and delivery. The probability that a woman will have a urinary tract infection during pregnancy is thus
    a. $0.04 \times 0.95 = 0.038$
    b. 0.05
    c. $0.04 + 0.05 = 0.09$
    d. $0.05 + (0.04)(0.95) = 0.088$
    e. $0.04 \times 0.05 = 0.002$
36. People with high levels of plasma high-density lipoprotein (HDL) cholesterol have been found to be at low risk for coronary heart disease. Factors associated with plasma HDL cholesterol were sought in a study of 293 healthy men. Table A2–2 shows the correlation coefficient and the *P* value associated with a test of zero correlation for plasma HDL cholesterol and each of the variables listed. All observations were taken at the same time for each of 293 participants.

Table A2–2 Correlations Between Plasma HDL Cholesterol and Five Variables

	r	P value
Plasma triglyceride	−0.42	<0.001
Alcohol intake	0.24	<0.001
Serum glucose	−0.19	<0.001
Body mass index	−0.11	>0.05
Diastolic blood pressure	−0.04	>0.05

Which of the following statements can be made regarding plasma triglyceride levels?

a. By increasing someone's plasma triglyceride levels, we can increase his plasma HDL cholesterol level.

b. By reducing someone's plasma triglyceride levels, we can increase his plasma HDL cholesterol level.

c. High levels of plasma HDL cholesterol tend to be found in men with low plasma triglyceride levels.

d. Low levels of plasma HDL cholesterol tend to be found in men with low plasma triglyceride levels.

e. The P value is too small to regard the correlation as anything other than a chance occurrence.

37. In a study of 50 cases of a disease and 50 controls, it is determined that the difference found with respect to a possible etiological factor is not statistically significant. One may conclude from this finding that

a. There is no association of the factor with the disease.

b. The difference may be clinically significant.

c. The difference may be the result of sampling variation.

d. The comparability of patients and controls has been confirmed.

e. Observer or interviewer bias has been eliminated.

38. At age 65, the probability of surviving for the next five years is 0.8 for a white male and 0.9 for a white female. For a married couple who are both white and age 65, the probability that the wife will be a living widow five years later is

a. 90%

b. 20%

c. 18%

d. 10%

e. 8%

39. The probability that at least one member of the couple will be surviving five years later is

a. 98%

b. 90%

c. 72%

d. 28%

e. 10%

40. A laboratory value with a mean of 18 g/dl and a standard deviation of 1.5 implies

   a. The true value is between 16.5 and 19.5 g/dl.

   b. The true value is between 15.0 and 21.0 g/dl.

   c. The error is too large for the determination to have any value.

   d. In repeated determinations on the same sample, 95% could be expected to fall between 15.0 and 21.0 g/dl.

   e. The true value has a 5% chance of being less than 16.5 or more than 19.5 g/dl.

41. Figure A2–1 is a scattergram that shows the relationship between systolic blood pressure (BP) and age in 33 women.

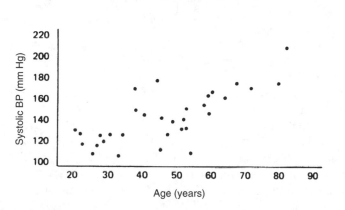

Figure A2–1 The Relation between Systolic Blood Pressure and Age in Women

Which of the following is the correlation coefficient between systolic blood pressure and age as determined from these data?

   a. +1.20

   b. –0.22

   c. +0.70

   d. –0.85

   e. 0

Questions 42 through 44 are based on the following study and its results in Table A2–3.

Table A2–3 Slope Coefficients Relating Gestational Period and Maternal Characteristics

Independent Variable	Slope Coefficient
Age (yr)	−0.0215
Height (in)	0.0279
Education (yr)	0.0424
Race (white = 0, black = 1)	−1.16
Number of previous pregnancies	0.0103

Intercept = 37.9
R^2 = 0.0242

A study of 833 pregnancies was used to obtain a multiple regression equation relating the gestational period in weeks to maternal characteristics.

42. The intercept indicates
    a. the mean gestation for this series of pregnancies
    b. the predicted gestation when all the independent variables have values of zero
    c. the earliest termination of pregnancy for this series
    d. the latest termination of pregnancy for this series
    e. the strength of the association between gestation and the five independent variables
43. The slope coefficient of −1.16 for race had a P value of less than 0.001; therefore, which of the following is true?
    a. The effect of race on gestation is likely to be the result of chance variation in the data.
    b. None of the variation in gestation can be attributed to the fact that both black and white women were included.
    c. All but 0.9% of the variation in gestation can be accounted for by race.
    d. A black woman is expected to give birth significantly earlier than a white woman with the same age, height, education, and number of previous pregnancies.
    e. The effect of race on gestation is probably because the blacks were different from the whites regarding age, height, education, and number of previous pregnancies.
44. In this series of pregnancies, age, height, education, race, and number of previous pregnancies
    a. provide a very accurate prediction of the length of gestation
    b. are unrelated to length of gestation
    c. are too variable to use as predictors of gestation

d. account for a large proportion of the variation in gestation

e. account for a small proportion of the variation in gestation

K-Type Questions

		Key		
a	b	c	d	e
1, 2, 3	1 and 3	2 and 4	only 4	all 4
are correct	are correct	are correct	is correct	are correct

45. When the distribution of a measurement in a healthy population is severely skewed, which of the following results?
    1. The normal range cannot be determined.
    2. The 2.5th and 97.5th percentiles are best determined from the cumulative distribution.
    3. The 2.5th and 97.5th percentiles are no longer the normal limits.
    4. The mean is distorted by extreme observations.

46. For a random sample of 500 schoolchildren in Baltimore City, 27% are found to be susceptible to measles. The standard error of the percentage susceptible is 2% . From this it is correct to conclude which of the following?
    1. The probability is 95% that the percentage susceptible for all schoolchildren in Baltimore City is between 25% and 29%.
    2. The sample is biased.
    3. The data should be age adjusted.
    4. The probability is 95% that the percentage susceptible for all schoolchildren in Baltimore City is between 23% and 31%.

47. Fifty known diabetics, all on insulin therapy, were compared with 50 nondiabetics. The diabetics showed a higher proportion of neurotic responses to a questionnaire ($P < 0.005$). This finding
    1. could be due to patient characteristics unrelated to diabetes
    2. may be influenced by the effects of insulin
    3. could occur if diabetes caused neurotic responses
    4. is likely to be a chance occurrence

48. In a diabetes detection program the screening level for blood glucose test A is set at 160 mg/dl and for test B at 130 mg/dl. This would mean that
    1. the sensitivity of test A is greater than that of test B
    2. the specificity of test A is greater than that of test B
    3. the number of false-positive results is greater with test A than with test B
    4. the number of false-negative results is greater with test A than with test B

49. As part of a routine physical examination, uric acid was measured for a 35-year-old male and found to be 7.8 mg/dl. The "normal range" for uric acid for

that laboratory is 3.4 to 7.5 mg/dl. If this individual does not display symptoms or signs of gout, the following may be cited as possible explanations:

1. He is among the small proportion of healthy individuals who yield high serum uric acid readings on a given test.
2. His level is within 2 standard deviations of the mean for healthy individuals.
3. His gout symptoms have not yet manifested themselves.
4. The departure of his level from the normal range is not statistically significant.

50. The following regression equation was developed from a study of 16 newly diagnosed diabetics who received phenformin for a period of one year:

$$L = -34 + 0.29 \, W$$

where L is the patient's weight loss one year after therapy began and W is the patient's initial weight. On the basis of this information we may conclude which of the following?

1. All patients lost at least 34 pounds during the first year of therapy.
2. The regression line fitted to a scattergram of weight lost versus initial weight would have a positive slope.
3. The correlation between weight loss and initial weight is positive and very strong.
4. Patients who weighed more than others at the beginning of therapy lost more weight, on the average, during the first year of therapy.

12

Case-Control (Retrospective) Studies

Objectives Covered

33. Distinguish between experimental and observational studies.
34. Describe a case-control (retrospective) study.

Study Notes

Experimental and Observational Studies

Experimental studies are the most easily recognizable because in these the investigator has control of some factor that, when varied, may be associated with different outcomes. Classically, this is usually seen in animal studies in which diet, for example, may be controlled and reproductive indices and growth rates measured. In human studies, however, ethical considerations limit the applicability of the experimental method and the investigator often must use the observational approach. Here, no manipulation is attempted, but differing outcomes are observed under natural conditions and related to differing exposures. People have some attribute, such as blood type A, or exposure, such as oral contraceptives usage, and the development of disease in the group with the attribute is compared with that in the group without. The difficulty is that the observed groups may differ in other ways in addition to the attribute in question, which may confound the comparison.

In order to label a study as experimental or observational, look for the hallmark of investigator control. If present, it signifies an experimental study. However, the majority of human studies are observational.

Sequence of Investigation for Etiology of Disease

First, the clinician makes an observation regarding cause, based on his or her experience. For example, in 1941, Gregg, an Australian ophthalmologist, reported a new syndrome of congenital cataract and linked it to rubella in the mother during pregnancy. Clinical observations such as this provide leads from which hypotheses are formulated. These hypotheses are then tested in sequence by case-control (retrospective) studies, and if the results are positive, by cohort (prospective) studies. Risk factors are then identified, and an intervention trial may be designed to ascertain if modification of such factors in patients is followed by a reduction in amount of disease.

Study Design

In the majority of epidemiological studies investigators have to complete the 2×2 table shown in Table 12–1.

"Exposure" is used here in a general sense, including the presence of an attribute such as hypertension, or any suspect etiological factor. "Disease" is used here, but it can include any outcome, such as survival.

If the approach is retrospective (Figure 12–1), the investigator starts with $a + c$ cases (Table 12–1). A comparison group of $b + d$ controls (see Table 12–1) is then selected, and the position shown in Table 12–2 is reached. Then a count of the numbers exposed and nonexposed in each group is determined (perhaps by interviews or record review) to complete the 2×2 table (see Table 12–1). Analysis is then performed by comparing the frequency of exposure between the case and control groups.

When the design is prospective, however, the investigator starts with the row total $a + b$ (the exposed group) and the row total $c + d$ (the nonexposed group), and the position shown in Table 12–3 is reached. The participants are then followed forward, and they eventually fall into the disease or nondisease columns, so the 2×2 table is completed prospectively (see Table 12–1). Analysis is then per-

---

Table 12–1 Sample 2×2 Table for Epidemiological Studies

		Disease	
		Present	Absent
Exposure	Present	a	b
	Absent	c	d

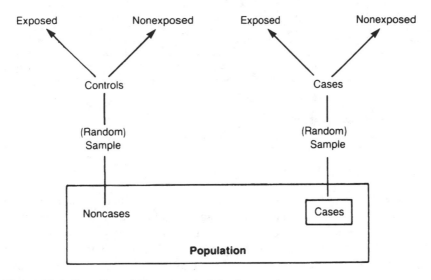

Figure 12–1 Case-Control (Retrospective) Study

formed by comparing the rate of disease occurrence (incidence) between the exposed and nonexposed groups.

The advantage of the case-control design is that it may be used to study a rare disease since cases may be collected retrospectively from the records of a group of large hospitals and compared with controls free of the disease. The prospective design, by contrast, entails assembling a study cohort, free of the disease under consideration, and following them forward in time so as to observe the development of the disease among some of their members. With a rare disease, however, the number of cases would be very small. Furthermore, the case-control study may yield a result in a relatively short time. This may be important if the outcome is a suspected pathologic process resulting from drug exposure. The price to be paid for these two advantages is that the probability of bias is greater in a retrospective study than in the prospective approach.

Table 12–2

		Disease	
		Present	*Absent*
	Present	?	?
Exposure	Absent	?	?
	Total	$a + c$	$b + d$

Table 12–3

		Disease		Totals
		Present	Absent	
Exposure	Present	?	?	$a + b$
	Absent	?	?	$c + d$

Bias

Bias is systematic error, resulting in overestimation or underestimation of the strength of the association. The validity of any study depends on the accuracy with which the subjects are assigned to the four categories: a, b, c, and d (see Table 12–1). Misclassification may occur because of overdiagnosis or underdiagnosis of disease. If a disease entity is well defined, such as cancer of the lung, the diagnosis is uniform and well established, the majority of cases come to medical attention, and there is little selectivity by physicians in hospitalizing the patient; misclassification is minimal.

Thromboembolic phenomena present a contrast. The disease is difficult to diagnose. It may present as a complication of another medical or surgical condition, and criteria are not uniform. Also the presence or absence of exposure may influence case management. If a young woman, known to be on oral contraceptives, presents with leg pain, she may be hospitalized more readily than another similar patient who is not on oral contraceptives. Thus, if case subjects and controls are ascertained via hospital records for a condition such as thromboembolic disease, it may be difficult to ensure they are representative of the situation in the community or that the two groups are comparable.

The sample of cases studied may not represent the entire spectrum of the disease. Hospitalized patients may exclude mild cases and those patients who die prior to admission. Coronary heart disease is such an example.

The design in Table 12–1 also assumes that the exposure is present or absent, both categories, of course, being mutually exclusive. The exposure may be difficult to define and measure (e.g., type A personality) or difficult to recall (e.g., drug use). Furthermore, the exposure may be intermittently present (e.g., oral contraceptive use). Thus, the row total $a + b$ may overrepresent or underrepresent the exposure in the sample. If the information sought is unchanging and usually available, such as blood group, bias may be minimal. In a more usual case, the needed information is not available and is sought by interview or questionnaire. The recall of events in the distant past may be inaccurate, or the information supplied by the informant may be biased.

Selective recall may occur among the cases, since they necessarily know they have the disease and may already associate it with exposure. The interviewer, being aware of the identity of cases and controls, may unconsciously probe more among the cases, seeking a positive association. To minimize bias from this source, the interviewer ideally should be unaware of which participant is a case or control, but this is difficult to achieve in retrospective studies.

Bias may occur in the selection of controls, particularly if hospitalized patients are used, as is frequently the case. It is essential that the control group be as much like the diseased group as possible, yet also similar to the general population in distribution of the exposure if the results are to be extended to the general population. The hospitalized controls may contain an unrepresentative proportion of a particular attribute (e.g., hypertensives and smokers).

Matching

The comparison between cases and controls may reveal a difference in exposure rates, and the development of disease may be ascribed to this difference, provided the two groups are otherwise comparable. In order to attain such comparability, they are frequently matched for characteristics already known to be strongly related to both disease and exposure. Age is frequently such a factor; therefore, in order to eliminate this effect from the comparison, the controls are matched to the cases for age. Socioeconomic status, because it influences environmental hazards and life styles and is associated with disease, is also used to match cases with controls. It should be emphasized that when a variable is used for matching, its etiologic role cannot be investigated because cases and controls are then automatically similar with respect to that characteristic. It is for this reason, and because matching often requires specialized (matched pair) analysis, that statistical adjustment (discussed in Chapters 2 and 11) during analysis is the preferred method of controlling for all but the strongest confounding factors.

Testing a Hypothesis

Let our hypothesis be that smoking is associated with lung cancer. Take 100 cases of lung cancer, and then choose 100 controls free of lung cancer from the general population, similar with regard to age, sex, and socioeconomic status; the resulting scale is shown in balance in Figure 12–2a. Now ascertain the smoking habits of the two groups; Figure 12–2b depicts the resulting imbalance. You have shown an *association* between smoking and lung cancer.

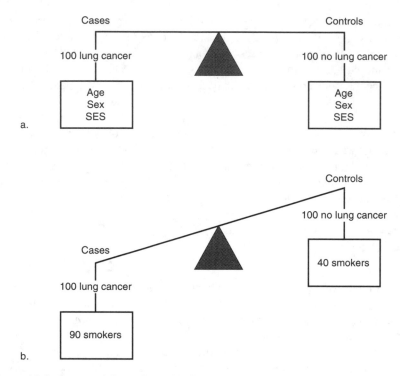

Figure 12–2 Cases and Controls are Similar with Regard to Age, Sex, and Socioeconomic Status (SES) (a) But Differ in Smoking Habits (b)

Analysis of Results

At the beginning of our study, the 2 × 2 table is only completed to the degree shown in Table 12–4.

During the study we retrospectively determine the number of smokers and nonsmokers in both the case and control groups. Thus, we find a, b, c, and d for the 2 × 2 table, as shown in Table 12–5.

Table 12–4

	Case Group	Control Group
Smokers	?	?
Nonsmokers	?	?
Total	100	100

Table 12–5

	Case Group	Control Group
Smokers	90	40
Nonsmokers	10	60
Total	100	100

Now we compare exposure rates for cases and controls, thus

$$\text{case exposure rate: } \frac{a}{a + c} = \frac{90}{100} \text{ or } 90\%$$

$$\text{control exposure rate: } \frac{b}{b + d} = \frac{40}{100} \text{ or } 40\%$$

$$P < 0.001$$

Statistical significance attached to the result is determined with a chi-square test, as described earlier. These analyses do not take into account any specific matching procedure (e.g., pairwise matching) that may have been used to make controls similar with respect to age, sex, and socioeconomic status. There are, however, techniques available to do this (see Hennekens and Buring in Recommended Readings).

Odds Ratio and Estimation of Relative Risk

Because of the case-control nature of the study, we cannot derive incidence for either the smokers or the nonsmokers. However, it is possible to estimate relative risk provided two assumptions are valid:

1. The disease has low incidence (5% or less) in the general population. (This is true for the majority of chronic diseases.)
2. The control group is representative of the general population with respect to the frequency of the exposure.

Under such circumstances a statistic called the odds ratio gives a close approximation to the relative risk:

$$\text{odds ratio} = \frac{ad}{bc}$$

In the example the odds ratio is

$$\frac{90 \times 60}{40 \times 10} = 13.5$$

and provides an estimate of the relative risk for smokers.

Exercises

In case-control studies:
1. a. **Your cases are 100 women with breast cancer. What is the essential prerequisite of the control group?**
   b. **Your hypothesis is that young age at first pregnancy is protective against breast cancer—should you match for socioeconomic status in cases and controls? Give your reasons.**
   c. **Is it possible to test the hypothesis that breast cancer rates are higher in single women than in married, using the same 100 cases and 100 controls?**
   d. **Suppose you found that 80% of the breast cancer cases were married; does this demonstrate that being married increases the risk of developing breast cancer?**
   e. **Assume that 90% of the control group are married. Estimate the relative risk of breast cancer for single women.**
2. **Your hypothesis is that alcoholics have an increased incidence of fatal automobile accidents. Design a case-control study to test this hypothesis using the following headings:**
   a. **Diagnosis of cases—difficult or not? Where would you find cases?**
   b. **Name a suitable population from which to choose controls.**
   c. **List matching characteristics for controls.**
   d. **What characteristic must you now determine for each study member?**
   e. **What difficulties might be encountered in determining this characteristic?**

Exercise Answers

1. a. **The controls should be free of breast cancer.**
   b. **Yes, socioeconomic status affects age at first pregnancy, so if you demonstrate an association, it may be due to socioeconomic status unless you matched for it.**

   c. Yes, but by indirectly using the odds ratio to estimate the relative risk.
   d. No, you need to compare this with frequency of marriage in the control group.
   e.

$$\text{Odds ratio} = \text{estimate of relative risk} = \frac{20 \times 90}{10 \times 80} = 2.25.$$

   (Derived from data in Table 12–6 below)

Table 12–6

	Cases	Controls
Single	20	10
Married	80	90
Total	100	100

2. a. Little difficulty in diagnosis of death from automobile accidents. You can find cases in the medical examiner's office and use police records to separate drivers from passengers.
   b. From motor vehicle records, identify other automobile drivers in the state who have not had fatal accidents. Notice that the controls should be drivers, since alcoholics may be overrepresented in the nondriving population, having lost their licenses.
   c. Age, sex, socioeconomic status (any characteristic that you think relevant to fatal automobile accidents may be used as a matching characteristic, but not alcohol use).
   d. Some measure of alcohol use.
   e. Alcohol use for deceased drivers might be difficult to ascertain, and control drivers may give false information on this point.

Reference

Gregg, N.M. 1941. Congenital cataract following German measles in the mother. Trans. Ophthalmol. Soc. Aust. 3:35.

Recommended Readings

Hennekens, C.H., and Buring, J.E. *Epidemiology in Medicine.* Edited by S.L. Mayrent. Boston, Little, Brown, & Co., 1987. Chapters 6 and 12 are a concise presentation of the major issues in the development and analysis of case-control studies, including the role of matching and adjustment to deal with confounding.

Hully, S.B., and Cummings, S.R. *Designing Clinical Research.* Baltimore, Williams & Wilkins, 1988. This book serves as a good how-to overview for those who are interested in doing case-control studies.

Lilienfeld, D.E., and Stolley P.D. *Foundations of Epidemiology,* 3rd ed. New York, Oxford University Press, 1994. Chapter 11 provides an informative discussion of the sources and effects of bias in case-control studies.

Schlesselman, J.J. *Case-Control Studies: Design, Conduct, and Analysis.* New York, Oxford University Press, 1982. This is an in-depth presentation of nearly all facets of epidemiological case-control studies.

13

Cohort (Prospective) Studies

Objectives Covered

35. Describe cohort (prospective) and cross-sectional studies.
36. Define *cohort,* and recognize a cohort effect when interpreting cross-sectional data.

Study Notes

Four different descriptive terms are used for prospective studies: *cohort, incidence, prospective,* and *longitudinal.* The four names of this type of study each emphasize a different aspect of the study. Cohort refers to the study group. Incidence refers to the fact that disease incidence (absolute risk) may be derived from this type of study, whereas it may not from a case-control study. Prospective refers to the fact that the study group is followed forward in time to the future from exposure to disease and is contrasted to case-control, which goes back in time to the past from disease to exposure. Longitudinal refers to the fact that study participants, once identified, are followed individually throughout the course of the study.

In a case control (retrospective) study, all of the relevant events (disease and exposure) have already occurred when the study is started. In a prospective study the exposure has occurred but the disease has not, except when the study is done entirely from records.

As can be seen from studying Figure 13–1, the investigator first assembles a group of volunteers (cohort) and examines them to make certain they are free of the disease in question at the start of the study. Numerous items of information (variables) are then collected, such as demographic, occupational, and medical data as well as social status. These variables must obviously include those that eventually prove relevant to the etiology of the disease. The cohort design, by its

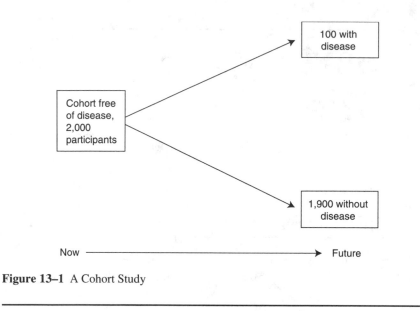

Figure 13–1 A Cohort Study

very nature, avoids two of the most potent causes of bias in the retrospective approach, namely the selection of controls and bias in ascertaining exposure. Controls are more appropriately and accurately defined as people who lack exposure. Because the exposure must necessarily occur prior to the development of the disease, there is less bias in ascertaining exposure: neither the observer nor the participants are prejudiced by prior knowledge of who has the disease and who has not.

One of the major limitations of the cohort approach stems from the fact that participants are frequently volunteers, and they must return at regular intervals to be examined for development of the disease and for variations in the exposure and other factors being monitored. Employed groups are frequently chosen because they are relatively easy to follow for some years. Railroad or government employees may be used, and such people differ both from the unemployed and from those in less secure occupations (e.g., salespeople, brokers, and many in entrepreneurial fields). The latter group may be exposed to more and different stresses, and the lure of the occupation may cause self-selection among its practitioners. The results of a study of an employed group are only strictly applicable to other similarly employed groups and are not necessarily generalizable to the population at large.

Thus, a cohort of healthy individuals is brought under observation and is classified with respect to the characteristics of interest (variables) to the investigator. If the rate of development of coronary heart disease (incidence) is to be studied, the cohort members are first examined to exclude those with preexisting coronary heart disease. The cohort is then kept under sufficient observation to identify those who develop the condition that is under study (in our example, coronary heart disease). In this way incidence rates for the disease may be developed for persons who are exposed and those who are not. To take another example, we might establish incidence rates of lung cancer over a 10-year period among persons categorized as smokers at the start of the period and contrast them to rates among nonsmokers.

Subjects Lost to Follow-Up

In cohort studies a small number of the group will be lost as the study ages year by year. It is generally assumed that the participants lost to follow-up have the same incidence of disease and the same outcome as those who remain under observation. This assumption may be fallacious if those who develop the disease may have migrated in order to obtain treatment, or they may move less than those remaining free of the disease, thus overstating the incidence of the disease in the latter event and understating it in the former. Attrition must be held to an acceptable minimum (generally not more than 10%) and must often be taken into account during analysis (see Chapter 15) in order for the conclusions from the study to remain valid. It is this constraint (attrition) that influences investigators to follow employed groups in preference to general population samples.

Analysis of Results

Consider a cohort of 2,000 people of whom 800 are smokers and 1,200 are nonsmokers. At the beginning of the study our 2×2 table is Table 13–1.

The entire cohort is observed for 20 years, and 100 participants develop lung cancer, of whom 90 are smokers and 10 are not. In Table 13–2 now we complete the 2×2 table.

Table 13–1 Cohort of 800 Smokers and 1,200 Nonsmokers

	Lung Cancer	No Lung Cancer	Totals
Smokers	a	b	800
Nonsmokers	c	d	1,200
Totals	a + c	b + d	2,000

Table 13–2

	Lung Cancer	No Lung Cancer	Totals
Smokers	90	710	800
Nonsmokers	10	1,190	1,200
Totals	100	1,900	2,000

We next compare incidence rates for smokers and nonsmokers:

$$\text{smokers: } \frac{a}{a+b} = \frac{90}{800} = 112.5 \text{ per } 1,000$$

$$\text{nonsmokers: } \frac{c}{c+d} = \frac{10}{1,200} = 8.3 \text{ per } 1,000$$

$$P < 0.001$$

Here again we determine statistical significance using a chi-square test.

Computation of Relative Risk

In a cohort study we are able to determine incidence rates directly in those exposed and those not. Thus, we calculate the relative risk as the ratio of the two incidences:

$$\text{relative risk} = \frac{a/(a+b)}{c/(c+d)}$$

In the example the relative risk is

$$\frac{90/800}{10/1,200} = 13.5$$

Comparison with Case-Control Studies (Table 13–3)

Case-control and cohort studies are usually not competing methods. Clinical observation or a prevalence survey (cross-sectional study) may provide the first suggestion of an association between exposure to a factor and development of disease. This hypothesis is then tested by means of a retrospective study. If the association is confirmed, a cohort study is often done. There are, however, circumstances in which the prospective approach is a more appropriate first design, as when the disease is as common as the exposure (e.g., the study of birth defects in infants born of diabetic mothers).

Table 13–3 Case-Control and Cohort Studies: Advantages and Disadvantages

Case-Control	*Cohort*
+ Short study time	− Long time required
+ Relatively inexpensive	− Very costly
+ Suitable for rare disease	− Relatively common diseases only
+ Ethical problems minimal	− Ethical problems may be considerable and influence study design
− Control group susceptible to bias in selection	+ Control group less susceptible to bias
+ Subjects need not volunteer (chart audit)	− Volunteers needed—results may not be generalized
− Biased recall possible	+ No recall necessary
+ Small number of subjects	− Large number of subjects
+ No attrition problems	− Attrition problems
− Cannot determine incidence	+ Incidence determined
− Relative risk approximate	+ Relative risk accurate

Nonconcurrent Cohort Study

The nonconcurrent (historical cohort) approach avoids many of the disadvantages of the prospective design. This occurs because it is done entirely or partially from existing records. For example, an investigator interested in lung cancer risks associated with exposure to a certain chemical might use employee records dating back to the 1950s to identify comparable employees who did and did not handle that chemical. By linking to personal and employee medical records as well as vital records, it may be possible to identify subjects among the exposed and nonexposed who developed lung cancer during the 30-plus years that have elapsed. The historical cohort approach takes advantage of the fact that all or many of the events of interest, including both exposure and disease, have already taken place at the outset of the study and thus avoids the costly longitudinal component. The price for this convenience is paid through both greater chances for bias, including in some instances uncertainty that exposure preceded disease, and potential knowledge of disease status when selecting for exposure. However, with some care and providence these problems may often be avoided and the nonconcurrent design may be a very effective tool.

Cohort

A cohort is a group of people who share a common experience within a defined time period.

A birth cohort is the most common example seen, but a cohort might be all those of one graduating class or survivors of myocardial infarction in one particular year. By following such a group forward for disease outcome, it is possible to distinguish between the influence of aging and underlying secular trends in the disease.

It is important to recognize a possible cohort effect in cross-sectional data, particularly in interpretation of survey data, which are commonly presented. An apparent trend shown in the cross-sectional data may be due to the cohort effect. For example, a study of a retrospective sample of general practitioners in North Carolina included, among other things, information on the number of medical journals subscribed to annually (Table 13–4). The inference that, as they grow older, general practitioners in North Carolina read fewer journals is incorrect because a cohort effect is operating. The trend toward reading fewer journals after age 50 is due to the presence, in that age group, of a cohort of physicians trained when fewer journals were published. In order to determine how reading habits vary with age, it is necessary to follow physicians' reading habits as they age.

Cross-Sectional Studies

Cross-sectional studies determine prevalence, not incidence. Their use is largely in prevalence determinations rather than in etiological investigation. For example, to ascertain the prevalence of hypertension in Baltimore City, the blood pressure of a sample of adult residents was taken in 1983. Other items of information gathered during the survey included age, sex, race, and occupation. Thus, we can determine how the prevalence of the condition is related to the variables measured. Such a study tells us about the distribution of a disease in the population, rather than its etiology. However, distribution patterns may suggest etiological hypotheses that can be tested by case-control studies and later by prospective studies.

Table 13–4 Number of Journals Subscribed to by General Practitioners in North Carolina

Age Group of Physicians	Number of Physicians	Mean Number of Journals Purchased
Under 30	4	4.5
30–39	34	4.2
40–49	27	4.6
50–59	21	3.6
60 and over	6	2.3

Exercises

1. **A cross-sectional study in 1976 revealed that the prevalence of oral contraceptive use varied with age, as shown in Table 13–5.**

Table 13–5 Prevalence of Oral Contraceptive Use

Age	Prevalence of Oral Contraceptive Use
15–19	15%
20–24	25%
25–29	22%
30–34	15%
35–39	7%
40–44	3%

The inference from these data that as women grow older they cease using oral contraceptives is
a. correct
b. incorrect because a rate is necessary to support the observation
c. incorrect because no control or comparison group is used
d. incorrect because a cohort effect may be operating
e. incorrect because prevalence is used whereas incidence is necessary

For questions 2 through 6, assign the studies described to one of the types listed below:
a. uncontrolled observation
b. cross-sectional or prevalence study
c. experiment
d. cohort study
e. case-control study

_____2. **Four rats in one cage were found dead at the university animal colony. In the adjacent cage, one rat convulsed and died, two rats became ill but survived, and one rat was ill. The veterinarian declared that an epizootic was present (epizootic—epidemic in animals).**

_____3. **Fifteen hundred adult males working for Lockheed Aircraft were initially examined in 1951 and were classified by diagnosis criteria** for coronary artery disease. Every three years they have been examined for new cases of this disease; attack rates in different subgroups have been computed annually.

_____4. A random sample of middle-age sedentary males was selected from four census tracts, and each man was examined for coronary artery disease. All those having the disease were excluded from the study. All others were randomly assigned to either an exercise group, which followed a two-year program of systematic exercise, or to a control group, which had no exercise program. Both groups were observed semiannually for any difference in incidence of coronary artery disease.

_____5. One hundred patients with infectious hepatitis and 100 matched neighborhood well controls were questioned regarding a history of eating raw clams or oysters within the preceding three months.

_____6. Questionnaires were mailed to every 10th person listed in the city telephone directory. Each person was asked to list age, sex, smoking habits, and respiratory symptoms during the preceding seven days. Over 90% of the questionnaires were completed and returned. Prevalence rates of upper respiratory symptoms were determined from the response.

Adenocarcinoma of the Vagina

Adenocarcinoma of the vagina in young women had rarely been recorded before the report of eight cases at the Vincent Memorial Hospital, Boston, between 1966 and 1969. The unusual occurrence of this tumor in eight patients born in New England hospitals between 1946 and 1951 led to an investigation. Attention was particularly directed at a history of maternal ingestion of estrogens during the pregnancy that resulted in the patient with vaginal adenocarcinoma.

7. What type of epidemiological study would be appropriate for this problem and why?

Exercise Answers

1. d. The inference may be true, but it cannot be derived from this cross-sectional data because of a possible cohort effect operating. It is necessary to follow a cohort forward in time and record the individuals' oral contraceptive use.

2. **a. uncontrolled observation**
3. **d. prospective study**
4. **c. experiment**
5. **e. case-control study**
6. **b. cross-sectional or prevalence study**
7. **A case-control (retrospective) or perhaps a nonconcurrent prospective study would be appropriate because**
   a. **the disease is very rare**
   b. **the diagnostic accuracy is high**
   c. **cases would not be missed**
   d. **the history of exposure to the suspected causative factor could be reliably obtained by history and/or records**
   e. **relative risk can be estimated.**

Recommended Readings

Breslow, N.E., and Day, N.E. *Statistical Methods in Cancer Research.* Vol. 2, *The Design and Analysis of Cohort Studies.* Lyon, International Agency for Research on Cancer, 1987. This text presents a very comprehensive treatment of the prospective studies, especially issues in analysis, for the more advanced student.

Hennekens, C.H., and Buring, J.E. *Epidemiology in Medicine.* Edited by S.L. Mayrent. Boston, Little, Brown, & Co., 1987. Chapter 7 presents a clear overview of the major issues of design, implementation, and analysis of prospective studies.

Hully, S.B., and Cummings, S.R. *Designing Clinical Research.* Baltimore, Williams & Wilkins, 1988. Several chapters in this book serve as a good how-to overview for those interested in doing cohort studies.

Lilienfeld, D.E., and Stolley, P.D. *Foundations of Epidemiology,* 3rd ed. New York, Oxford University Press, 1994. Chapter 10 provides further discussion of both concurrent and nonconcurrent approaches with good examples of each.

14
Randomized Clinical Trials

Objective Covered

37. Describe a randomized clinical trial.

Study Notes

The experiment is the strongest weapon in the scientific armamentarium to test a hypothesis. In the physical sciences the experimental method is ordinarily chosen. Animal experiments are common in biology, but when human subjects are involved, opportunities for experimentation are limited.

The purposes of the retrospective and prospective studies described in Chapters 12 and 13 has been to identify the etiology of disease. The experimental intervention studies now described usually have a different primary purpose, namely to determine which is superior among competing treatments (Figure 14 1). Nevertheless information gained from experiments may be useful in confirming etiological relationships suggested by observational studies. For example, knowledge that smoking cessation programs for pregnant women are effective in the prevention of low birth weight infants adds strong support for the conclusion that smoking during pregnancy is a cause of low birth weight.

As in observational cohort studies, clinical trials are prospective, that is, the entire group of participants must be followed and monitored for outcome. The major distinction is that the investigator manipulates or intervenes with one group and withholds intervention from another, the control group. This is in contrast to the studies previously described, which have been observational, where the investigator merely observes and takes no action. Random allocation of patients to various treatment groups is the hallmark and is "pathognomonic" of clinical trials.

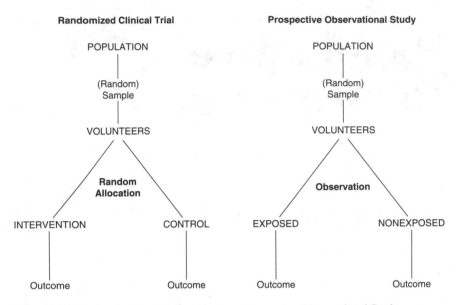

Figure 14–1 A Randomized Clinical Trial vs. Prospective Observational Study

Informed Consent

The fact that intervention is applied to one group and withheld from another means that the participants must all be volunteers. Those asked to participate are usually at high risk for the outcome of interest (e.g., myocardial infarction, preterm delivery, or fetus with neural tube defect). The request for informed consent spells out this fact, and the patient is permitted to question the interviewer administering the consent form. Regardless of whether the patient consents or declines to participate, his or her behavior may be modified in light of the knowledge of high-risk status and appreciation that this risk can be lowered. Despite this limitation, the randomized trial yields results that cannot be obtained by any other method.

Random Allocation of Study Subjects

Random assignment of study participants to intervention and control groups is the procedure that will give the greatest confidence that the groups are comparable (i.e., alike at the beginning of the trial). This is true for risk factors, both known and unknown, and is the crucial point to be grasped in the design of these trials. If you have two groups of patients, and you apply a different treatment to each group, you can only ascribe a difference in outcome to the differing treatment if that is the only factor that differs between the groups; this situation can only be achieved if group membership is determined randomly. Because of the similarity in terms it is important to distinguish between random selection of study subjects from a population, which may occur in both observational studies and experiments, and the subsequent random allocation of subjects to intervention and nonintervention groups (see Figure 14–1), which only occurs in experiments. The process of randomization is alien to the clinician, whose training and practice correctly emphasize discrimination, selection, and judgment prior to instituting treatment.

Elimination of Bias

Both investigator and participant are subjected to the influence of their respective expectations as to the efficacy of the treatment. In order to reduce bias from this source, blinding techniques are used. In double blinding, neither the subject nor the investigator knows to which group the subject is assigned. This technique is most desirable in trials where subjective end points, such as "improved," "unchanged," or "worse," are used. If objective end points, such as death or stroke, are measured, blinding is not essential.

Placebo Effect

A well-known phenomenon in medicine is that patients given only inert substances (e.g., sugar pills) will often show subsequent clinical improvement when compared with similar patients not so "treated." This phenomenon, termed the *placebo effect,* must be taken into account in clinical trial design if effects in the intervention group are to be ascribed to the intervention itself and not to the generic effect of being treated. The usual method to accomplish this is to use an inert treatment that is indistinguishable from the primary intervention in the control group. Thus, the only difference between groups is the specific intervention under study.

Analysis

There is usually a predictable sequence to clinical trial analysis. It begins with a comparison of the intervention and control groups to demonstrate comparability (that randomization worked). This includes comparisons of such factors as age, sex, race, and especially known risk factors not under study. It is followed by an analysis to demonstrate that the intervention worked (e.g., that antismoking intervention did result in lower tobacco use in the intervention group). Finally, the main analysis to test whether the hypothesized health effect resulted (e.g., lower respiratory tract cancer risk) is performed.

In principle, the main analysis of clinical trials does not differ greatly from the analysis of observational cohort studies except in some subtle ways. For instance, in the clinical trial it is not necessary that the intervention be successfully implemented in every member of the intervention group (e.g., all stop smoking) and be universally absent in the controls (e.g., none stop smoking), only that a substantial difference be achieved (e.g., reduced tobacco consumption in the intervention group). Furthermore, the main analysis should be based on the "intention to treat" principle; that is, once subjects are allocated to a group, they should be retained as assigned for the main analysis. Otherwise if subjects are selectively excluded from analysis the benefits conferred by random allocation are at least partially sacrificed. Thus, the "golden rule" of clinical trials is that "everyone randomized is analyzed." While follow-up losses owing to patient dropout are not excluded from this rule, there are circumstances in which moderate losses cannot be avoided and may often be handled using one or more survival analysis methods (see Chapter 15).

Exercises

A randomized clinical trial, referred to as the University Group Diabetes Program (UGDP) was performed to evaluate different methods of treatment of diabetes.

The principal features of this clinical trial included the establishment of a common protocol for the collection of comparable data, random allocation of patients to treatment groups, the inclusion of a comparable placebo-treated group, double-blind evaluation of the oral drugs, long-term observation of patients, and central collection, editing, and monitoring of the study data. The patients selected for the UGDP had non-insulin dependent diabetes mellitus (NIDDM) and did not require insulin to remain symptom free. This type of diabetic constitutes the majority (over 90%) of the diabetic population.

1. **How did the selection of this type of diabetic affect the applicability of any conclusions derived from this trial?**
2. **When is double-blind evaluation most necessary? Least necessary? What does it involve?**

The UGDP had two major objectives:

1. Evaluation of the efficacy of hypoglycemic treatments in the prevention of vascular complications in a long-term, prospective, and cooperative clinical trial
2. Study of the natural history of vascular disease in NIDDM

The following therapy regimens were studied in the UGDP:

I. Insulin variable (IVAR): insulin is given in varying amounts in order to maintain normal blood glucose levels
II. Insulin standard (ISTD): insulin lente U-80 is given in doses ranging from 10 to 16 units per day depending on body surface
III. Tolbutamide (TOLB): 1.5 g/day orally
IV. Lactose placebo (PLBO): in forms and dosage schedules corresponding to those used for the oral hypoglycemia agents

All groups received the same diet prescription.

Results

The researchers reached several surprising conclusions:

1. Insulin (in either dosage) is no more effective than diet alone in prolonging life among patients with NIDDM.
2. Diet plus tolbutamide, the most commonly used oral hypoglycemic agent, is no more effective than diet alone in prolonging life in patients with NIDDM.
3. There is a statistically significant excess of cardiovascular deaths among the tolbutamide group compared with the placebo group.

Some results are expressed in Figure 14–2.

3. **Was it ethical to treat one group with a placebo?**
4. **Today it would be more difficult to carry out such a trial. Why?**
5. **If no placebo group had been included, which conclusions would be lost?**

Beginning in 1961 patients were recruited in 12 clinical centers. The four treatment groups contained a total of 1,027 patients. All patients were assigned randomly to one of the four treatment groups.

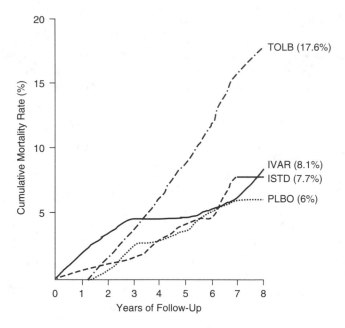

Figure 14–2 Cumulative Mortality Rates per 100 Population at Risk by Year of Follow-Up. Cardiovascular Causes of Death Only. *Source:* Modified from Klimt et al., 1970

---

6. Why is randomization essential and what does it accomplish?

Exercise Answers

1. **Any results from this study, as with any other study, are only applicable to populations similar to the study population. In this instance, however, this is not a constraint because the patients studied were representative of a large cross-section of patients with NIDDM.**
2. **Double-blind evaluation is necessary to eliminate subjective bias by observers and subjects. It is most necessary when the outcome is subjective, such as "improved," "unchanged," or "worse." It is least necessary for an objective end point, such as "death." It involves blinding subjects and investigators to treatment/placebo assignment.**
3. **Informed consent was obtained from all participants, who were very closely monitored for any untoward effects. Prominent diabetologists involved in the design of the trial believed that the placebo group might fare as well as the other groups, and that belief was justified.**

4. Today this trial may not have received clearance from an ethical viewpoint, i.e., the Human Volunteers Committee, because of the inclusion of the placebo group.
5. The most important conclusions would not have been reached if the placebo had been dropped, that is,
   a) that insulin is not superior to placebo
   b) that tolbutamide is associated with increased risk of death due to cardiovascular causes (statistically significant) compared with the placebo.
6. Randomization is essential because then and only then can the difference in outcome between the groups be ascribed to the treatment applied. If randomization is omitted, the difference in outcome may be due to differing characteristics in the competing groups. Randomization achieves an unbiased distribution of risk factors (e.g., age, sex, severity of disease). This principle is the underlying concept on which randomized clinical trials are based.

Reference

Klimt, C.R., Knatterud, G.L., Meinert, C.L., and Prout, T.E. 1970. University Group Diabetes Program: A study of the effects of hypoglycemic agents on vascular complications in patients with adult onset diabetes. *Diabetes* 19 (suppl. 2):747.

Recommended Readings

Fletcher, R.H., Fletcher, S.W., and Wagner, E.H. *Clinical Epidemiology: The Essentials.* Baltimore, Williams & Wilkins, 1982. Chapter 12 presents an excellent example and detailed analysis of the UGDP clinical trial.

Hennekens, C.H., and Buring, J.E. *Epidemiology in Medicine.* Edited by S.L. Mayrent. Boston, Little, Brown & Co., 1987. Chapter 8 presents a more in-depth overview of the major issues of design, implementation, and analysis of clinical trials.

Hully, S.B., and Cummings, S.R. *Designing Clinical Research.* Baltimore, Williams & Wilkins, 1988. Several chapters in this book serve as a good how-to overview for those interested in doing experimental research.

Mausner, J.S., and Kramer, S. *Mausner and Bahn: Epidemiology—An Introductory Text,* 2d ed. Philadelphia, W.B. Saunders Co., 1985. Chapter 8 emphasizes design as well as different types of experiments.

Meinert, C.L. *Clinical Trials: Design, Conduct, and Analysis.* New York, Oxford University Press, 1986. This text presents a very complete treatment of issues of the design, analysis, and implementation of clinical trials.

15

Survival Analysis

Objectives Covered

38. Describe the circumstances that require prospective studies to control for differences in time under observation.
39. Describe how the following methods control for differences in time under observation, and indicate what assumptions underlie each:
    a. Person-time
    b. Life table, Kaplan-Meier analysis
40. Describe the role of proportional hazards methods in survival analysis.

Study Notes

Uneven observation of study subjects is a common problem with which even well-designed prospective studies must contend. The free entry and withdrawal of human subjects in a prospective study results in variation of follow-up times that must be dealt with during analysis. The principal methods used to accomplish this are outlined below. While these procedures were first developed for the analysis of survival time, they are applicable to other time dependent outcomes as well, provided the underlying assumptions are met.

Published data (Miller, 1981) on the survival of patients undergoing heart transplantation at Stanford University are illustrative of the problem. Information collected on 65 patients included survival status, age at time of surgery, a donor-recipient tissue mismatch score (T5), donor heart rejection status, and survival time. These data might be used to examine the question of whether subjects with low mismatch scores (low T5 $\leq$ 1.1) have better survival than those with high mismatch scores (high T5 > 1.1).

On first consideration, the investigator might perform a conventional relative risk analysis (Table 15–1) to investigate this question. Such an analysis offers little support for the hypothesized association; however it ignores the potential for unequal time under observation (follow-up) between the groups. A slightly deeper examination of the data reveals a substantial difference in mean follow-up times

Table 15–1 Conventional Relative Risk Analysis of Heart Transplant Survival

Level of Tissue Mismatch	Number of Subjects	Mortality		Relative Risk of Mortality
		Number	Percent	
High	32	23	72	1.31
Low	33	18	55	

between the groups (low T5 = 477 days; high T5 = 286 days). This difference needs to be taken into account in the analysis. The person-time approach is one method to accomplish this.

Person-Time Approach

Person-time is computed as the sum of individual follow-up times or for grouped data as the product of group size and the average duration of observation. Applying this approach to the above problem yields the results in Table 15–2.

Table 15–2 Person-Years Analysis of Stanford University Heart Transplant Study

Tissue Mismatch	Deaths	Person-Years	Death Rate per Person-Year	Relative Risk
High	23	23.05	0.92	2.21
Low	18	43.38	0.41	

Once average differences in time under observation have been taken into account, there appears to be considerable support for the hypothesis that tissue mismatch is related to the risk of mortality after transplant surgery.

Person-time analysis assumes that the two components (numbers of persons and follow-up time) contribute equally to health event rates. This implies for example that 10 persons observed for 1 year and 1 person observed for 10 years provide equivalent information for the assessment of health outcomes (i.e., each would contribute 10 person-years of observation). This will usually only be true if the risk of the study event is uniform over the interval(s) analyzed. It is difficult to check adherence to this assumption in the summary analysis above because we have ignored the intermediate results that would indicate the pattern in mortality over time. We could subdivide the person-years analysis into shorter time periods, but this is also the foundation of life table analysis, which offers some other advantages.

Life Table Analysis

The life table method attempts to equalize time effects through stratification, that is, subdividing the interval of observation into smaller periods to permit the estimation of the probability of the outcome of interest, frequently mortality, during each period among those alive at the start of each period. The periods should be small enough so that the outcome of interest as well as the entry of new subjects and withdrawals are uniform across the period. The other major assumption is that those censored prior to death (or other outcome of interest) experience the same risk of death as those who continue. *Censoring* refers to the inability to follow all subjects until they reach the study end point. It arises when subjects withdraw or are lost from follow-up before the completion of the study or when subjects could not have received equivalent observation because they were enrolled at different times (e.g., as in the study of the first several patients undergoing heart transplant surgery).

The standard cohort life table analyses for these data are presented in Table 15–3. The "adjusted number at risk column" is used to control for additions or losses of subjects during an interval.

It is computed as follows:

$$\text{alive at start of interval } - \frac{\text{censored during interval}}{2}$$

e.g., using line 1 of Table 15–3,

$$33 - \frac{3}{2} = 31.5$$

Since these events are assumed to be random and thus equally probable at any point during the period, on average subjects lost or added are considered to be under observation for half the period. By extension participants who enter and leave during the same period are considered on average to be under observation for one-fourth of the period. No adjustments are made during the period for subjects who "die" because they are not censored (i.e., they have been followed to the study outcome). However, deaths as well as losses are eliminated from the next period, while new entrants are added to those under observation during the next

Table 15–3 Life Table Analysis of Heart Transplant Survival

Start of Interval (Months)	Alive at Start of Interval	Changed Status during Interval		Adjusted Number at Risk	Estimated Probability of Death in Interval	Estimated Probability of Surviving to Interval
		Dead	Censored			
Cohort 1—Low Tissue Mismatch Score						
0	33	5	3	31.5	0.159	1.000
2	25	4	0	25.0	0.160	0.841
3	21	2	1	20.5	0.098	0.707
7	18	3	3	16.5	0.182	0.638
13	12	2	1	11.5	0.174	0.522
25	9	1	2	8.0	0.125	0.431
37	6	1	5	3.5	0.286	0.377
49	0					0.269
Cohort 2—High Tissue Mismatch Score						
0	32	4	0	32.0	0.125	1.000
2	28	6	0	28.0	0.214	0.875
3	22	7	1	21.5	0.326	0.688
7	14	2	0	14.0	0.143	0.464
13	12	1	6	9.0	0.111	0.397
25	5	2	1	4.5	0.444	0.353
37	2	0	1	1.5	0.000	0.196
49	1					0.196

period. Each subsequent period is adjusted in like fashion to compute the probability of "death." The estimated probability of survival to each interval is computed as the product of probabilities of surviving (1 − probability of dying) each preceding interval and is used to construct the survival curve (Figure 15–1). Refer to Chapter 6 for a fuller description of computations involving probabilities.

The life table analyses reveal more clearly the pattern of mortality and the character of any groupwise differences. While there is no groupwise difference in mortality in the short term following surgery, survival appears to fall more precipitously in the high mismatch group and remains depressed throughout the period of observation. Notice that there is considerable variation in the risk estimate across the time intervals studied. This variation violates the requirement for constant risk across the interval analyzed and thus calls into question the results of the summary person-years analysis. It emphasizes the need to define shorter intervals for analysis whenever such variability occurs.

An extension of this concept, the product-limit or Kaplan-Meier life table (not illustrated), chooses life table intervals so small (e.g., days) that it is unnecessary to perform "at risk" adjustments. It is especially advantageous for small samples

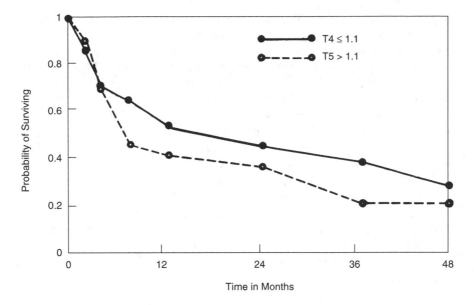

Figure 15–1 Life Table Probability of Surviving Heart Transplant Surgery

because each subject's exact survival time is used, and thus it provides more information and improved statistical power than the standard life table method. The probability of "death" is computed as the fraction of deaths among all those alive at the start of the interval. Intervals with no deaths are ignored because they do not change survival. The only underlying assumption is that subjects who withdraw experience the same risk as continued participants.

Thus far, analyses have ignored effects of confounding factors. Such effects could be taken into account in the above analyses by first stratifying the data by the levels of the confounding variable and performing person-time or life table analyses within each stratum and then combining results across strata. However, these methods are arduous and do not make maximal use of the data. As in other such problems, computerized multiple regression models have become the method of choice.

Proportional Hazard Models

The Cox proportional hazards approach employs regression analysis of study data to predict for each subject the time to the study end point. It controls for both differential time under observation as well as differences in subject characteristics (e.g., age, race, sex). Although a Cox regression equation can be used to obtain the probability that a given subject will reach the end point by a specified time, interest usually centers on the slope coefficients. The slope coefficients in the Cox regression equation can be translated into relative risks (for the end point) associated with various levels of the independent variables. As always, in the context of regression, the relative risk found for a particular independent variable is adjusted for all the other independent variables.

Underlying this method is the assumption that a basic prediction model can be used to estimate each subject's survival time across the entire period of observation. It further assumes a constant relative risk over time associated with each of the independent variables in the model.

When a Cox regression model was fitted to the data with only the tissue mismatch factor included as an independent variable, a relative risk of 1.6 was estimated for the high compared with the low mismatch group. When age was included as a second independent variable the relative risk for high tissue mismatch was estimated at 1.7. This indicates that age is not an important confounding variable in these data.

Exercises

1. **Refer to Tables A1–4 and A1–5 and questions 17 and 18 on pages 43 and 44. Assume these data were compiled within two weeks of the occasion when the foods being analyzed were consumed. None of the survival analyses methods were applied to estimate the risk or probability of disease associated with consumption of various foods. Was that appropriate? Justify your answer. In general, when is it necessary to take time into account in disease risk analysis?**

For each situation described below in questions 2 through 6, determine which of the following methods of analysis is most appropriate:

a. Relative risk A $= \dfrac{\text{Rate per 1,000 people exposed}}{\text{Rate per 1,000 people unexposed}}$

b. Relative risk B $= \dfrac{\text{Rate per 1,000 person-years exposed}}{\text{Rate per 1,000 person-years unexposed}}$

c. Standard life table

d. Kaplan-Meier life table

e. Cox regression

_____2. Comparison of the prevalence of major hearing deficit measured by standardized audiography in employees of two new machine shops, one with a modern sound dampening design (shop A), the other without (shop B). Assume employees of the two shops are similar except for the time of the audiograms, which are done at one year after employment in shop B and at one and one-half years in shop A.

_____3. Comparison of the survival of two small but highly comparable groups of patients having similar surgery performed in two centers but with different techniques.

_____4. Comparison of the incidence of myocardial infarction or sudden death among citizens grouped by baseline diastolic blood pressure levels and followed in annual examinations for the next 10 years. Assume that subjects differ in age, education, and income and that not all subjects keep their appointments for annual physical examinations.

_____5. Comparison of the risk of total mortality in two comparable communities during the same calendar year.

_____6. Comparison of the survival of two large, randomly allocated groups of patients with high serum cholesterol levels, one receiving lovastatin and the other cholestyramine treatments for lowering cholesterol. Expect treatment withdrawals not to be rare.

7. Under what circumstances is it possible for person-years and life table analyses to produce different summary relative risk estimates?

8. The following table of relative risks were computed as the ratio of probabilities of mortality in the high T5 compared with the low T5 groups for each interval in Table 15–3.

Start of Period (Months)	Relative Risk of Death in High T5 vs. Low T5 Group
0	0.79
2	1.34
3	3.33
7	0.79
13	0.88
25	3.55
37	0.00

What do these results suggest concerning the assumptions underlying Cox regression?

Exercise Answers

1. Survival methods are not necessary because the observation time is equal in the groups being compared.
2. b. Person-time is appropriate because the groups differ only in time under observation, there is only one assessment of the outcome, and the risk of the outcome should be relatively constant over the period of exposure.
3. d. Kaplan-Meier is most appropriate because the detailed data necessary to perform life table analysis will be present, the sample size is small, and the groups are comparable.
4. e. Cox regression is the best choice because it will perform a detailed analysis of events during the period of observation and will permit the investigator simultaneously to control for effects of factors on which the subjects are known to differ.
5. a. Standard relative risk analysis is appropriate because follow-up time is equal. In two comparable communities follow-up losses are likely to be similar and small relative to the population-sized groups being compared.
6. c. Standard life table analyses are appropriate to control for the differences in follow-up time likely to arise if withdrawals are "not rare." Cox regression is not necessary because subjects were randomly allocated to the two groups and thus should be similar in other characteristics. The large sample size makes it unnecessary to perform the more arduous Kaplan-Meier analysis.
7. Person-years can produce a distorted picture whenever risk varies substantially within the interval used for analysis.
8. The relative risks vary across periods of analysis. This violates the proportional hazards assumption of a constant relative risk over time for each independent variable. Thus the summary relative risk arising from Cox regression would have to be interpreted with care.

Reference

Miller, R.G., Jr. 1981. *Survival Analysis.* New York, John Wiley & Sons.

Recommended Reading

Kahn, H.A., and Sempos, C.T. *Statistical Methods in Epidemiology.* New York, Oxford University Press, 1989. Chapters 7 and 8 provide a more in-depth discussion of each of the topics presented here, including significance testing and details on the implementation of each method with several examples.

16

Association and Causation

Objectives Covered

41. Illustrate with one example the concept of multifactorial causation of disease.
42. Define the following types of association:
    a. artifactual
    b. noncausal
    c. causal
43. Distinguish between association and causation, and list five criteria that support a causal inference.

Study Notes

Epidemiologic studies yield statistical associations between a disease and exposure. This is only the first step. We must interpret the meaning of these relationships. An association may be artifactual, noncausal, or causal.

An artifactual or spurious association may arise because of bias in the study. Sources of bias are discussed in Chapter 12. Noncausal associations occur in two ways:

1. The disease may cause the exposure (rather than the exposure causing the disease).
2. The disease and the exposure are both associated with a third (confounding) factor, X, known or unknown (see Figure 16–1). Here, in measuring exposure we are inadvertently measuring X.

An example of the second type of noncausal association follows. A positive statistical association between coronary heart disease (CHD) mortality rates and

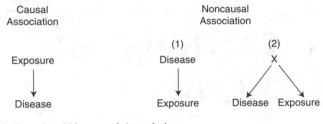

Causal Association	Noncausal Association	
	(1)	(2)
Exposure	Disease	X
↓	↓	↙ ↘
Disease	Exposure	Disease Exposure

Figure 16–1 Causal and Noncausal Associations

coffee drinking habits has been demonstrated. Let us assume the results shown in Table 16–1.

Table 16–1

Coffee Consumption (Cups per Day)	CHD Mortality in Males Aged 55–64 (Deaths per 1,000 per Year)
0	6
1–5	8
6+	12

However, it has been shown that people who drink coffee also tend to be cigarette smokers, and cigarette smoking is strongly associated with CHD mortality, as shown in Table 16–2.

Thus, to isolate the effect of coffee drinking, we cross-classify CHD mortality rates according to both variables (Table 16–3). Examination of Table 16–3 reveals that when cigarette consumption is held constant, the effect of coffee drinking disappears. Thus, the association between coffee drinking and CHD mortality is noncausal, mediated by the confounding factor cigarette smoking (Figure 16–2). This means that if coffee drinking is varied independently of cigarette consumption, CHD mortality rates are unchanged.

Table 16–2

Cigarette Consumption (Packs per Day)	CHD Mortality in Males Aged 55–64 (Deaths per 1,000 per Year)
0	4
1–2	10
3+	15

Table 16–3

Coffee	CHD Mortality Rates			
	Cigarettes (Packs per Day)			
(Cups per Day)	0	1–2	3+	All
0	4	9	15	6
1–5	6	10	13	8
6+	5	9	16	12
All	4	10	15	

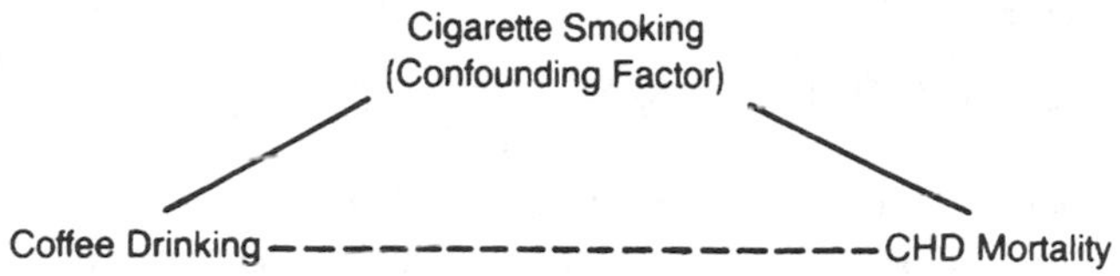

Figure 16–2 Noncausal Association between Coffee Drinking and CHD Mortality

Multiple Causation

When an outcome is affected by multiple variables, in order to examine the influence of a single one, it is necessary to adjust for the effects of the others. An earlier example is the use of age adjustment to control for the effects of age on mortality. A simple technique for isolating a specific effect due to one variable is to examine the outcome rates, at several levels of this variable, while holding the other variables constant. This technique is cross-classification. A sophisticated approach involves the use of multiple regression analysis to measure the effect of the relative contribution of each of a series of variables on an outcome.

Medicine offers numerous examples of multiple causation. Maternal mortality, for example, is affected positively by both age and parity (number of children born). It is necessary to study women of certain parity, for example, 1, 2–3, 4–5, and 6+, and in each of these four groups examine the relationship between age and maternal mortality. The result will be that the age effect persists in all parity groups, and the effect is very marked. If women in age groups <20, 20–29, 30–39, and 40+ are classified according to parity within each of the age groups, it will be found that increasing parity is associated with a small increase in maternal mortality, but not nearly as marked an effect as that of age.

Causal Association

Medicine is concerned with limiting or preventing disease. The search for etiology is pursued in the hope that, once the cause of a disease is found, prevention will follow. Causality is assumed when one factor is shown to contribute to the development of disease and its removal is shown to reduce the frequency of disease. This concept of causality is different from that applied in law or philosophy. In prevention, it is sufficient to identify an exposure without necessarily identifying the ultimate cause of the disease. For example, cigarette smoke has been identified as the contaminated substance that is associated with increased rates of lung and other cancers as well as heart and respiratory diseases. It is unnecessary to identify precisely which component in the smoke is the prime offender before instituting preventive measures.

Establishing Causation

Statistical methods alone cannot establish proof of a causal relationship in an association. Interpretation of such an association must be conducted in a systematic manner (Figure 16–3).

The advisory committee to the Surgeon General of the Public Health Service (Advisory Committee, 1964) defined five criteria that should be fulfilled to establish a causal relationship. These five criteria have been generally adopted as a test of causation. They are

1. consistency of the association
2. strength of the association

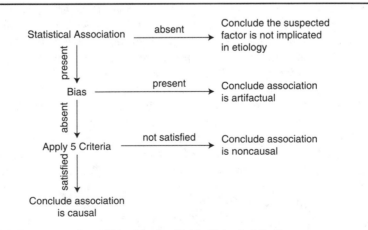

Figure 16–3 Interpretation of Results of an Epidemiological Study

3. specificity of the association
4. temporal relationship of the association
5. coherence of the association

The definitions are summarized below:

1. Consistency means that different studies resulted in the same association, despite the fact that they employed different designs and were conducted on different populations, sometimes in different countries.
2. Strength refers to the size of the relative risk found. The greater the relative risk, the more convincing it is that the association is causal. Furthermore, if a dose-response gradient can be demonstrated, the likelihood that the exposure is causal increases. Such dose-response gradients may be recorded as the degree (e.g., the number of cigarettes smoked daily) or duration of exposure (e.g., the length of time for which oral contraceptives have been used).
3. Specificity measures the degree to which one particular exposure produces one specific disease. If the biological response to the exposure is variable, it is less likely to be causal.
4. Temporal relationship means exposure to the factor must precede development of the disease.
5. Coherence means biological plausibility, which may have been established in animal models.

The five criteria quoted above are the best guide to etiology in the absence of a controlled experiment, but they cannot be considered to be a substitute for the latter.

Exercises

1. **Tables 16–4, 16–5, and 16–6 give the results of a study of the factors associated with response to a cervical cancer screening program.**
   From these data it would be correct to infer that
   a. **Married women respond better.**
   b. **No inferences can be drawn from these tables because the marital status of high and low social class people is not shown.**
   c. **Married people have a higher response rate than do the single or widowed because more of them are in a high social class.**
   d. **No inference can be drawn from these tables because it is not known if this is a cohort or case-control study.**

Table 16–4 Response to Program by Social Class

Social Class	Percent Population Responding
High social class	75
Low social class	46
All social classes	53

Table 16–5 Response to Program by Marital Status

Marital Status	Percent Population Responding
Married	82
Single	68
Widowed and divorced	43
All marital status	53

Table 16–6 Percent of Persons in Each Subgroup (Social Class by Marital Status) Responding to Program

Social Class	Married	Single	Widowed and/or Divorced	All Marital Status
High social class	83	67	43	75
Low social class	81	69	43	46
All social classes	82	68	43	53

2. **Table 16–7 shows the data obtained in a cross-sectional study of obesity and blood pressure.**
    From these data, which of the following conclusions may be correct:
    a. **50/100 = 50% of those with intermediate blood pressure are obese.**
    b. **100/1,000 = 10% of those with high blood pressure are obese.**
    c. **50/200 = 25% of the obese have low blood pressure.**
    d. **100/500 = 20% of those with high blood pressure are thin.**

Table 16–7 Relationship of Obesity to Level of Blood Pressure (Expressed as Numbers of People)

	Low Blood Pressure	Intermediate Blood Pressure	High Blood Pressure	Total
Obese	50	50	100	200
Normal weight	170	30	100	300
Thin (nonobese)	380	20	100	500
Total	600	100	300	1,000

3. The association between cigarette smoking and lung cancer has been subjected to considerable scrutiny. Which of the following statements both strengthen the association between cigarette smoking and lung cancer and move the evidence toward the direction of a causal relationship?
   a. The risk of lung cancer increases as the daily consumption of cigarettes increases and/or as the duration of smoking lengthens.
   b. Ex-smokers have lung cancer incidence rates intermediate between those of nonsmokers and current smokers.
   c. Animal experiments have shown an increased incidence of precancerous lesions following tobacco smoke inhalation.
   d. Prospective studies agree with retrospective studies about the presence and direction of the association.
4. Retrospective studies have shown a higher level of stress reported by survivors than reported by controls in the year prior to a heart attack. Can it be concluded from this study that stress causes heart attacks?
5. Cross-sectional studies (surveys) reveal that a higher proportion of Arizona residents have respiratory disease than residents of other states. Can it be concluded from this that living in Arizona causes respiratory disease?
6. A study of stillbirths and congenital malformations revealed that a higher proportion of mothers of such children had taken steroids during pregnancy than a control group of mothers of normal children. From this information, may we conclude that taking steroids during pregnancy causes stillbirths and congenital malformations?

Exercise Answers

1. a. Married women respond better regardless of social class. Table 16–4 seems to indicate that the response is associated with social class.

Table 16–5 seems to indicate that the response is associated with marital status. However, Table 16–6 reveals that if social class is held constant, the influence of marital status persists, but that if marital status is held constant, the influence of social class disappears.

2. a and c are correct.

3. a, b, c, and d are all correct.

4. No. It is unclear if stress caused the heart attack or if the heart attack caused the stress or some other unknown factor caused both. The question must be examined prospectively.

5. Not necessarily. Those with respiratory disease may have migrated to Arizona because of the climate.

6. Not necessarily. The difficulty with such studies is that the steroids may have been prescribed because of a history of bleeding or contractions during pregnancy or for mothers with a poor obstetrical history. The association may be noncausal.

Reference

Advisory Committee to the Surgeon General of the Public Health Service, 1964. *Smoking and Health.* P.H.S. Publication No. 1103, pp. 182–189. Public Health Service, Washington, D.C.

Recommended Readings

Hennekens, C.H., and Buring, J.E. *Epidemiology in Medicine.* Edited by S.L. Mayrent. Boston, Little, Brown, & Co., 1987. Chapter 8 provides an overview of association and causation with an excellent example using smoking and lung cancer.

Susser, M. *Causal Thinking in the Health Sciences: Concepts and Strategies in Epidemiology.* New York, Oxford University Press, 1973. The entire book is devoted to the concept of causality and the principles of establishing cause in epidemiological investigations.

17

Keys To Understanding Articles on Epidemiologic Studies

Objectives Covered

44. Use the abstract of a journal article from the medical literature to create an overview that lists the study type, indicates the principal findings, and highlights the potential pitfalls.
45. Use the overview as a guide for the critical examination of the report.

Study Notes

Establishing an Overview of the Report

This chapter presents a method for systematically examining a journal article. The method starts with step 1, the examination of the abstract of the paper to create an overview. The overview will serve as a "map" to guide the reader's focus during step 2, the reading of the paper itself. Step 3 will focus on making the determination of whether the results are valid and, if so, how widely they can be applied. An example at the end of the chapter illustrates the application of the procedure to an actual abstract taken from the medical literature.

Exhibit 17–1 outlines the content of the overview in step 1, which involves: (1) generating a basic description of the study and its findings, and (2) identifying critical issues to consider in judging the credibility of the findings. To begin, read the abstract of the paper and complete items I through III to describe the purpose, design, and results of the study. Next, use the table in item IV to determine the methodologic issues that typically apply to the study type established in item II. Each of the items in the overview is discussed more fully below.

Exhibit 17–1 Outline of the Overview of the Report

I.   Purpose of Study

A.   Nature of the effect being studied:

Exposure _____

Outcome _____

B.   Target population (check one):

___ General   ___ Specific _____
                                                    (describe)

II.   Study Type

Which best describes the type of study involved (check one):

___ Clinical Trial (RCT)   ___ Cohort (COH)

___ Case-Control (C-C)   ___ Cross-Sectional (C-S)

III.   Findings

A.   Results regarding effect of exposure:

B.   Conclusions:

IV.   Issues for Critical Reading

Potential Problem	Implication	Source of Problem	Code	RCT	COH	C-C	C-S
Unfair comparison	Result biased/ Misleading	Confounding	1		x	x	x
		Differential attrition	2	x	x		
		Unequal ascertainment					
		Exposure	3			x	x
		Outcome	4	x	x		x
Deficient ascertainment	Effect underestimated	Exposure determination					
		Contrast diluted	5	x			
		Poor indicator	6	x	x	x	x
		Misclassification	7	x	x	x	x
		Outcome determination					
		Poor indicator	8	x	x	x	x
		Misclassification	9	x	x	x	x
Unrepresentative sample	Limited application	Restricted selection	10	x	x	x	x
		Selective attrition	11	x	x		

Purpose of the Study

Recall, from the earlier chapters, that most epidemiologic studies can be visualized in terms of a 2×2 table. The skeleton of the table in Exhibit 17–1 is meant to bring this picture to mind. The ultimate purpose of most studies is to measure the effect of an exposure (e.g., smoking during pregnancy) on an outcome (e.g., low infant weight). Both the exposure and the outcome are often identified in the title of the paper. If not, the abstract should certainly identify them.

It is important to recognize the target population to which results will be applied. Sometimes this target population will be mentioned in the report. When the target population is not explicitly identified, it can often be inferred from the exposure or the outcome. For example, with a study intended to examine the effect of smoking during pregnancy, the target population would be pregnant women. If no target population can be identified, assume that the results are meant to apply to the general human population.

Methodologic Features of the Study

The most important aspect of the methodology is whether the study is experimental or observational, i.e., whether the exposure for any given subject is determined by a mechanism under the investigator's control. The most common type of experimental epidemiologic study is the randomized clinical trial (RCT). Here the investigator uses randomization to allocate subjects to the study groups. Notice that experiments have the ability to establish the temporal sequence from exposure to outcome. Likewise, observational studies can be classified according to whether the investigator actually observes the natural history of exposure followed by outcome. With a cohort study it is usually observed and with a case-control study it is not. A study that documents this sequence is in a stronger position to infer causality.

Among the three main kinds of epidemiologic studies, it is generally recognized that the clinical trial provides the strongest evidence of causation, and the case-control the weakest. The cohort study falls in between, but ranks nearer the case-control study than the clinical trial in the hierarchy.

An observational study that determines both the exposure and the outcome at the same point in time is referred to as a cross-sectional study or prevalence survey. While this type of study is neither retrospective nor prospective, it is usually regarded as closest to the case-control study in terms of strength of evidence for causation. From a cross-sectional study, investigators sometimes report a prevalence ratio (the prevalence of the outcome for those exposed divided by the prevalence for those not exposed). This should not be interpreted as a relative risk. The prevalence ratio is influenced by factors other than those involved in the etiology.

For example, when the outcome is the presence of a health condition or chronic disease, a prevalence ratio greater than one could arise because those exposed have access to better medical care and therefore survive longer than those not exposed.

Findings

The abstract contains results that summarize the association between the exposure and the outcome. Look for statistics such as odds ratios or relative risks that indicate the magnitude of the apparent effect. When the outcome is measured quantitatively, as with birth weight, for example, the difference in means for the exposed and nonexposed groups indicates the apparent effect of exposure. When, in addition to having a quantitative outcome measure, the study has a quantitative measure of exposure (e.g., number of cigarettes smoked during pregnancy), the correlation coefficient might be presented.

Remember that, while these statistics may indicate an effect of exposure, the reader should always be ready to question their precision. Look for P values to establish statistical significance. Look for confidence intervals (CIs) to establish a range of effect sizes that is compatible with the data.

Finally, identify the conclusion drawn by the investigators regarding the effect of the exposure and its implications from a clinical or public health point of view.

Issues for Critical Reading

Having gleaned the most important information available in the abstract, the reader is now ready in step 2 to focus on identifying problematic aspects of the study and its findings. Such matters can only be fully addressed by a careful reading of the article itself. However, it behooves even the most casual reader to be aware of problems that could affect the validity of the conclusions.

All studies are susceptible to three general kinds of pitfalls. In order of importance, these are: (1) unfair comparisons, (2) deficiencies in the ascertainment of the exposure and/or the outcome, and (3) unrepresentative sampling. Part IV in Exhibit 17–1 indicates the implications of these general problems and the flaws that frequently cause them. A code number is assigned to each for future reference. The last four columns under part IV indicate (by the Xs) those study types that are the most vulnerable to each specific flaw.

Ultimately, it is important in step 3 to assess the validity and generalizability of the results. Figure 17–1 is meant to assist the reader in using the overview to make these decisions. First, it helps to prioritize the issues in part IV of Exhibit 17–1 to identify studies that are likely to mislead. Here we differentiate studies likely to yield wrong conclusions from studies likely to correctly assess the presence of an effect but to underestimate its magnitude. The former may lead to erroneous decisions, whereas the latter probably will not. Second, among those studies that are

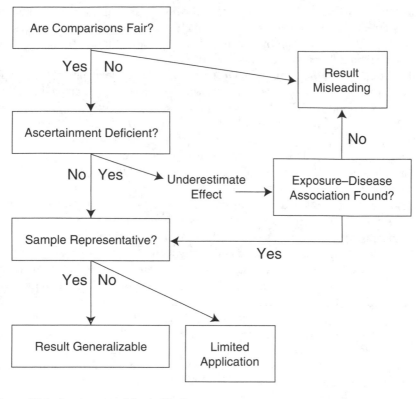

Figure 17-1 Assessment of Study Findings

considered valid, it focuses on the applicability (generalizability) of the results. With this in mind, we will review each of the potential pitfalls and the study flaws that cause them.

Unfair Comparisons

Unfair comparison occurs when study groups differ at the outset due to confounding (code #1) or experience differential attrition (code #2), or suffer from unequal ascertainment of exposure (code #3) or outcome (code #4). Confounding arises when factors related to the outcome of interest are not balanced across groups being compared. For example, in a study of myocardial infarction (MI) in patients with high- and low-cholesterol levels, the groups are likely to differ also on age, because cholesterol levels tend to rise with age. Therefore, since MI increases with age it is necessary to balance age in the two groups by matching or statistical adjustment so that the estimate of MI risk is not influenced also by the age difference. This problem is common to all studies except RCTs in which the groups are likely to be approximately balanced on all confounders (known and unknown) through random allocation.

Differential attrition occurs when losses from different segments of the sample are not balanced across the study groups. This is more likely to happen in follow-up studies (cohort or RCT), but case-control and cross-sectional studies are also susceptible. If patients with side effects but no perceived benefit drop out of the intervention group but not the control group, the intervention will appear more effective than it actually is. Nonparticipation at the outset, due to subject refusals or other reasons, may also lead to unfair comparisons if the reason is related both to the exposure and the outcome. For example, refusal rates are often higher for cases than for controls in a case-control study because of disease-related impairment. If the most impaired cases are the ones most likely to be exposed (i.e., exposure increases the severity, as well as the risk of the disease, the association between exposure and disease will be underestimated).

To indicate that the groups available for analysis are relatively free of distortion due to attrition, comparisons are sometimes provided on sociodemographic and other variables. In the absence of such a demonstration, equality of attrition rates across groups does not imply comparability. Maintenance of a low-attrition rate is the best insurance against these problems. If more than 30% of the subjects originally selected for study are lost, there is reason for concern.

Each study type is vulnerable to certain biases in ascertaining the exposure and/ or the outcome. The prospective studies, including RCT and cohort, are liable to bias in ascertaining disease outcomes (e.g., a study of the association of a self-reported illness with a well-publicized environmental exposure may lead to over-reporting of disease in the group aware of its exposure). The case-control study is especially susceptible to recall bias (e.g., greater "soul searching" regarding exposures during pregnancy in women who delivered a malformed baby than among control women delivered of a normal baby). The cross-sectional study that ascertains both exposure and disease is susceptible to both.

Blinding (masking) is used to prevent biased ascertainment (see Chapter 14). While it might be found in any type of study, it is most commonly a feature of the RCT in which the identity of the intervention is disclosed to neither the subjects nor the observers.

Deficient Ascertainment

Deficient ascertainment refers to problems related to defining and measuring the exposure and the outcome. In almost all instances, this causes inaccuracies that result in an underestimate of the effect size. Thus, this problem is more important to consider for negative studies, i.e., those failing to report an association between exposure and disease (see Figure 17–1).

The diluted contrast problem (code #5) relates mainly to the RCT. It occurs when there is poor compliance with the intervention (e.g., if the intervention is a drug that has unpleasant side effects and therefore is not taken according to protocol). It also occurs when the control group becomes excessively "contaminated." For example, in a clinical trial of smoking cessation, the control group would be contaminated by subjects that quit smoking. This would be a serious problem if the quit rates for the comparison groups become too similar.

A poor indicator of exposure (code #6) or outcome (code #8) arises when an operational definition is used that only weakly reflects reality. For example, occupational health studies sometimes use job type as a proxy for exposure to toxic agents (e.g., pipe fitter to infer lead exposure). Similarly, adverse health outcomes in such studies are often inferred from work absenteeism.

Misclassification of study subjects by the exposure (code #7) or the outcome (code #9) can arise even when their definitions do not involve proxy indicators. When a study relies on self-reports of exposure (e.g., alcohol consumption) or outcome (e.g., automobile accidents), misclassification can be a serious problem unless an independent source can be found for confirmation.

Unrepresentative Samples

An unrepresentative sample refers to a study sample that differs from the target population to such an extent that study results may not apply. This situation may arise in any study because the initial selection of participants is too restrictive (code #10) (e.g., selecting only hospitalized cases and controls to study a condition such as hypertension with a relatively low-hospitalization rate). Notice that this would omit all but the most severe cases.

Even after the initial selection, the sample can become unrepresentative due to selective attrition (code #11), that is, unequal loss according to characteristics (e.g., age) of the study subjects. This can occur in any type of study due to nonparticipation of certain segments of the sample. It can also occur in cohort studies or RCTs due to follow-up losses, which are more frequent in certain kinds of subjects. For example, in a cohort study, economic and other barriers may cause subjects from lower socioeconomic strata to decline participation in higher numbers and to drop out at higher rates.

Critical Examination of the Report

In moving from the overview to the article itself, the reader is advised to play the role of a juror trying to reach a verdict in a case of law. Weigh the evidence and attempt to draw your own conclusions. The evidence includes: the success of the study in avoiding the methodologic pitfalls identified by the overview, the quality of the presentation and interpretation of the data, and the compatibility of the findings with previous knowledge.

Avoidance of Pitfalls

In order of importance, in step 2 the reader should assess to what extent the study is affected by unfair comparisons, deficient ascertainment, and unrepresentative samples. Figure 17–1 presents a decision chart to help the reader use this information in step 3 to reach a conclusion about the validity and generalizability of the findings.

The problem of unfair comparisons is, by far, the most serious. Unless the investigators are successful in countering this problem, the results will be misleading. Techniques for this purpose include design features such as randomization, matching, and blinding, as well as analytical methods such as stratification and regression modeling.

Deficient ascertainment almost always serves to weaken results. In a negative study (one reporting no association between exposure and disease) this is a serious problem that may invalidate the results and conclusions. In a positive study, nonbiased deficiencies in ascertainment serve to reduce the apparent magnitude of the effect and therefore render the findings more conservative, but they do not generally lead to wrong conclusions regarding the presence of an association.

Unrepresentative sampling may limit generalization of study findings. Rather than being applicable to the entire target population, the result can only be applied safely to a particular segment of the target population. Nevertheless, it still could represent an important advance of knowledge.

Quality of the Report

Does the report help the reader to evaluate the credibility of the findings presented? All participants who entered the study should be enumerated and an accounting should be provided for those not included in the analysis. Each table and figure should have a clear role in the interpretation of the data. Numerical inconsistencies should be explained.

A well-written article will be forthcoming about the limitations of the study and provide enough detail to enable the reader to recognize them. Sometimes the limitations are described explicitly in the discussion section. Although the quality of the study, and hence the credibility of its findings, should not be confused with the quality of the report, these attributes are often congruent.

Compatibility with Previous Knowledge

How well do the findings fit into the spectrum of results from other studies in this area? Although most articles will provide such a comparison in the discussion section, without knowing the literature the reader is at a distinct disadvantage. Incompatibilities should be addressed by the author. The reader should evaluate the plausibility of these arguments, keeping in mind that the author, rather than some disinterested party, has chosen the results to cite and the issues to emphasize.

Example

Presented below is an example of the application of this procedure to create an overview of the abstract in Exhibit 17–2. The completed overview is included as Exhibit 17–3. This is followed by an illustration of how the overview can be used to help frame the review of the article itself. While the article is not included, Figure 17–2 provides a diagram that highlights the main features of the study. (The reader is encouraged to obtain and read the article itself.) Exhibit 17–4 presents a critical assessment of the report in terms of avoidance of pitfalls, quality of report, and compatibility with previous findings, with a final summary based on Figure 17–1.

Exhibit 17–2 Example Abstract from *New England Journal of Medicine*

The Absence of a Relation between the Periconceptional Use of Vitamins and Neural-Tube Defects

James L. Mills, M.D., M.S., George G. Rhoads, M.D., M.P.H., Joe Leigh Simpson, M.D., George C. Cunningham, M.D., Mary R. Conley, M.A., Melinda R. Lassman, M.A., M.S., Margaret E. Walden, B.A., O. Richard Depp, M.D., Howard J. Hoffman, M.A., and the National Institute of Child Health and Human Development Neural Tube Defects Study Group

Whether taking multivitamins or folate around the time of conception can reduce a woman's risk of having a child with a neural-tube defect is controversial. To investigate this question, we examined the periconceptional use of vitamin supplements by women who had a conceptus with a neural-tube defect (n = 571), women who had had a stillbirth or a conceptus with another malformation (n = 546), and women who had had a normal conceptus (n = 573). Women with conceptuses with neural-tube defects were identified either prenatally or postnatally and were matched to control mothers for gestational age. To minimize recall bias, we interviewed nearly all the women within five months of the diagnosis of a birth defect or the birth of the infant (mean, 84 days); information on vitamin use was obtained by an interviewer who was unaware of the outcome of pregnancy.

The rate of periconceptional multivitamin use among the mothers of infants with neural-tube defects (15.8 percent) was not significantly different from the rate among mothers in either the abnormal or the normal control group (14.1 percent and 15.9 percent, respectively). After adjustment for potential confounding factors, the odds ratio for having an infant with a neural-tube defect among women classified as having had full supplementation with multivitamins was 0.95 as compared with the mothers of the abnormal infants (95 percent confidence interval, 0.78 to 1.14) and 1.00 as compared with the mothers of normal infants (95 percent confidence interval, 0.83 to 1.20). There were no differences among the groups in the use of folate supplements. The adjusted odds ratio for having an infant with a neural-tube defect among those receiving the recommended daily allowance of folate was 0.97 as compared with the mothers of abnormal infants (95 percent confidence interval, 0.79 to 1.18) and 0.98 as compared with the mothers of normal infants (95 percent confidence interval, 0.80 to 1.20).

We conclude that the periconceptional use of multivitamins or folate-containing supplements by American women does not decrease the risk of having an infant with a neural-tube defect.

Source: Reprinted from Mills, J.L., Rhoads, G.G., Simpson, J.L., et al. The absence of a relation between the periconceptional use of vitamins and neural-tube defects, *New England Journal of Medicine,* Vol. 321, pp. 430–435, 1989.

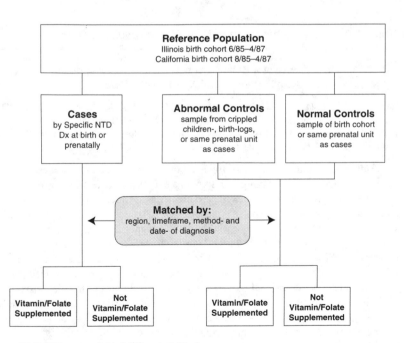

Figure 17-2 Diagram of the Mills, et al Study

Exhibit 17–3 Step 1—Completed Overview of the Report in Exhibit 17–2.

I. **Purpose of Study**

	OUTCOME	
	+	−
EXPOSURE +		
−		

A. Nature of the effect being studied:

Exposure <u>Periconceptional use of multivitamins containing folic acid</u>

Outcome <u>Neural-tube defects (NTD)</u>

B. Target population (check one):

___ General __x__ Specific ____<u>Women of childbearing age</u>____
(describe)

II. **Study Type**

Which best describes the type of study involved (check one):

___ Clinical Trial (RCT) ___ Cohort (COH)

__x__ Case-Control (C-C) ___ Cross-Sectional (C-S)

III. **Findings**

A. Results regarding effect of exposure:

After adjustment for potential confounders, the odds of having an infant with an NTD were 0.97 (95% CI 0.79–1.18) in women classified according to folate intake as meeting the recommended daily allowance for folic acid. Similar results obtain for women classified as fully supplemented.

B. Conclusions:

No association between multivitamin use around the time of conception and having a baby with an NTD

IV. **Issues for Critical Reading** (*indicates relevant codes for present study)

Potential Problem	Implication	Source of Problem	Code	RCT	COH	C-C	C-S
					Studies Most Vulnerable		
Unfair comparison	Result biased/ misleading	Confounding	1*		x	x	x
		Differential attrition	2	x	x		
		Unequal ascertainment					
		Exposure	3*			x	x
		Outcome	4	x	x		x
Deficient ascertainment	Effect underestimated	Exposure determination					
		Contrast diluted	5	x			
		Poor indicator	6*	x	x	x	x
		Misclassification	7*	x	x	x	x
		Outcome determination					
		Poor indicator	8*	x	x	x	x
		Misclassification	9*	x	x	x	x
Unrepresentative sample	Limited application	Restricted selection	10*	x	x	x	x
		Selective attrition	11	x	x		

Exhibit 17–4 Step 2—Critical Examination of the Report

Avoidance of Pitfalls (numbers in parentheses refer to codes in Part IV of Exhibit 17–1)

The cases were drawn from residents of California and Illinois, populations with relatively low risk of NTD (10). A relatively low response rate with 30%–40% of selected subjects being nonparticipants created the potential for both selective and differential losses among study groups (2,11). The demonstrated sociodemographic similarity of participating cases and controls mitigates some but not all of the concern over differential losses. Losses as great as 30%–40% leave too much room for hidden biases to have an impact. Confounding due to differences in sociodemographic factors or healthy behavior was minimized both by matching on race/ethnicity, region, time, method and date of diagnosis, and statistical adjustment using multiple logistic regression (1). A number of efforts were directed at reducing unequal ascertainment of exposure including the use of an abnormal control group to reduce recall bias, short lag time between diagnosis and interview, and blind ascertainment of medical and exposure history during the periconceptional period (6,7). Clear definition of NTDs based on the presence of defects at birth or on prenatal ultrasound with confirmation, clear definition of exposure based on use of multivitamins or certain supplemented cereals, and short lag time between diagnosis and interview reduced risk of deficient ascertainment (6-9). However, failure to assess dietary folate other than fortified cereal could lead to under ascertainment of exposure (7).

Quality of Report

Tables are logical, informative, clearly labeled, and numerically consistent. The investigators describe a number of possible limitations of the study including potential for self-selection bias due to nonrandom assignment of vitamin/cereal use, and potential for incomplete ascertainment of NTDs with the possibility of the failure to include a folate susceptible subgroup. They also note that their study population represented a relatively low-risk group for NTDs, and the possibility that higher risk populations may include vitamin-preventable NTDs not included in the present study. However, they do not address the issue of incomplete ascertainment of dietary folate and other vitamins.

Compatibility with Previous Knowledge

Mills, et al compare their results to the main published data: an Atlanta case-control study and small clinical trials in Britain. They correctly describe the greater risk of recall bias in the Atlanta study, which assessed vitamin use 2.5–16 years after study births, and mention but fail to identify methodologic problems with the British trials.

continues

Summary (Step 3)

The Mills, et al study is generally well-designed and the report is informative. Nevertheless, there are two important problems: relatively large losses of subjects between selection and interview, and failure to assess dietary (noncereal) sources of folate and other vitamins. Using Figure 17–1, the first raises the possibility of unfair comparison, mitigated somewhat by the demonstrated similarity of the study groups. The second raises the concern of deficient ascertainment, which could render the study incapable of finding a real association. Another potential problem is the use of a relatively low-risk population that may fail to include risk factors present in one at higher risk. These considerations lead us to regard the study as flawed and at least potentially misleading, and therefore to withhold judgment on this issue pending review of other studies.

Exercises

1. **Review the following abstract and prepare the overview according to the criteria in Exhibit 17–1.**

Multivitamin/Folic Acid Supplementation in Early Pregnancy Reduces the Prevalence of Neural Tube Defects

Aubrey Milunsky, MBBCh, Dsc, FRCP, DCH; Hershel Jick, MD; Susan S. Jick, MPH; Carol L. Bruell, MS; Dean S. McLaughlin, PhD; Kenneth J. Rothman, DrPH; Walter Willett, MD

We examined the relation of multivitamin intake in general, and folic acid in particular, to the risk of neural tube defects in a cohort of 23,491 women undergoing maternal serum a-fetoprotein screening or amniocentesis around 16 weeks of gestation. Complete questionnaires and subsequent pregnancy outcome information was obtained in 22,776 pregnancies, 49 of which ended in a neural tube defect. The prevalence of neural tube defect was 3.5 per 1000 among women who never used multivitamins before or after conception or who used multivitamins before conception only. The prevalence of neural tube defects for women who used folic acid-containing multivitamins during the first 6 weeks of pregnancy was substantially lower—0.9 per 1000 (prevalence ratio, 0.27; 95% confidence interval, 0.12 to 0.59 compared with never users). For women who used multivitamins without folic acid during the first 6 weeks of pregnancy and women who

continues

used multivitamins containing folic acid beginning after 7 or more weeks of pregnancy, the prevalences were similar to that of the nonusers and the prevalence ratios were close to 1.0.

Source: Reprinted from Milunsky, A., Jick, H., Jick, S.S., Bruell, C.L., McLaughlin, D.C., Rothman, K.J., and Willett, W., Multivitamin/folic Acid Supplementation in Early Pregnancy Reduces the Prevalence of Neural Tube Defects, *Journal of the American Medical Association,* Vol. 202, pp. 2847–2852, with permission of the American Medical Association, 1989.

2. **Review the following abstract and prepare the overview according to the criteria in Figure 17–1. Use that along with the original article (not provided) to develop a critical evaluation of the report.**

Prevention of Neural Tube Defects: Results of the Medical Research Council Vitamin Study: MRC Vitamin Study Research Group

A randomized double-blind prevention trial with a factorial design was conducted at 33 centers in seven countries to determine whether supplementation with folic acid (one of the vitamins in the B group) or a mixture of seven other vitamins (A, D, B_1, B_2, B_6, C, and nicotinamide) around the time of conception can prevent neural tube defects (anencephaly, spina bifida, encephalocele). A total of 1817 women at high risk of having a pregnancy with a neural tube defect, because of a previous affected pregnancy, were allocated at random to one of four groups— namely, folic acid, other vitamins, both, or neither. 1195 had a completed pregnancy in which the fetus or infant was known to have or not have a neural tube defect, 27 of these had a known neural tube defect, 6 in the folic acid groups and 21 in the two other groups, a 72% protective effect (relative risk 0.28, 95% confidence interval 0.12–0.71). The other vitamins showed no significant protective effect (relative risk 0.80, 95% CI 0.32–1.72). There was no demonstrable harm from the folic acid supplementation, though the ability of the study to detect rare or slight adverse effects was limited. Folic acid supplementation starting before pregnancy can now be firmly recommended for all women who have had an affected pregnancy, and public health measures should be taken to ensure that the diet of all women who may bear children contains an adequate amount of folic acid.

Source: Reprinted from MRC Vitamin Study Research Group, Prevention of Neural Tube Defects: Results of the Medical Research Council Vitamin Study, *Lancet,* Vol. 338, pp. 131–137, with permission of Lancet Ltd., © 1989.

Exercise Answers

1. Exposure - Periconceptional Multivitamins/Folic Acid
   Outcome - Neural-Tube Defect (NTD)
   Specific Target Population - Women of Childbearing Age
   Method - Cohort Study
   Result: Prevalence of NTD was 0.27 (95% CI 0.12-0.59) times as
                 low in women taking compared to not taking folic acid con-
                 taining vitamins during the first 6 weeks of pregnancy.
   Conclusion: Evidence is consistent with the inference that folate or an-
                 other substance in multivitamins is protective against
                 NTDs.
   Issues for critical reading by code no: 1, 2, 4, 6–11.

2. Exposure - Periconceptional Multivitamins and/or Folic Acid
   Outcome - Neural-Tube Defect (NTD)
   Specific Target Population - Women of Childbearing Age
   Method - Multicenter, Randomized Clinical Trial
   Result: Prevalence of NTD was 0.28 (95% CI 0.12–0.71) times as
                 low in women taking compared to not taking folic acid (but
                 not other vitamins) around the time of conception.
   Conclusion: Evidence strongly supports the inference that folic acid is
                 protective against NTDs.
   Issues for critical reading by code no: 2, 4–11.

   Critical Examination of the Report:

   The sample was representative of high-risk women who had previously
   given birth to a fetus with NTD (10). Attrition (failure to provide an informative pregnancy) was similar across study groups and by clinical
   center, but high (~25%) due to the early termination of the trial. While
   there was no table showing comparability of the groups analyzed on
   baseline criteria, the paper does provide a comparison of uninformative
   outcomes (miscarriages, ectopic pregnancies, termination of pregnancies) to show that they were comparable across study groups (11, 2). All
   pregnancy outcomes were examined, and specific neural-tube defects
   were diagnosed at participating centers, and confirmed based on review
   of clinical or necropsy material by experts blinded to group assignment
   (4, 8, 9). Compliance with vitamin use was monitored by pill counts and
   serum folic acid levels among study groups that showed a marked contrast in levels between four groups which included all possible combinations of using and not using folic acid and nonfolic acid–containing vitamins (5–7). The protective effect of folic acid was so great that the trial

had to be stopped early because it would not have been ethical to withhold supplementation from patients in the nonfolic acid groups. In spite of the high doses used, there were no serious side effects reported. This was a thorough, well-designed, and well-conducted study, which led to the recommendation in the United States that all women of childbearing age consume 0.4 mg of folic acid per day in order to greatly reduce their risk of conceiving babies with NTDs.

Recommended Readings

Medical Epidemiology. Edited by R.S. Greenberg. Norwalk, Appleton and Lange, 1993. Chapter 11 features interpretation of the epidemiologic literature with an example regarding diet and breast cancer.

Dawson-Saunders, B., and Trapp, R.G. *Basic and Clinical Biostatistics.* Norwalk, Appleton and Lange, 1994. Chapter 15 is devoted to the application of biostatistical concepts in reading the medical literature.

Riegelman, R.K., and Hirsch, R.P. *Studying a Study and Testing a Test: How To Read the Medical Literature.* 2d. ed. Boston, Little, Brown and Company, 1989. Part 1 is a highly readable discussion of the issues relating to design, conduct, and analysis of epidemiologic studies; especially useful are the flaw-catching exercises.

Self-Assessment 3

Objectives Covered: 33–45

Best Choice—Select *One* Answer Only

51. In a cross-sectional study of peptic ulcer in a community, people meeting the symptomatic criteria for peptic ulcer were found in 80 per 100,000 men aged 35 to 49 and 90 per 100,000 women aged 35 to 49. The inference that in this age group, women are at greater risk of developing peptic ulcer is
    a. correct
    b. incorrect due to failure to distinguish between incidence and prevalence
    c. incorrect because rates were used to compare males and females
    d. incorrect due to failure to recognize a possible cohort effect
    e. incorrect because there is no comparison or control group

52. Epidemiologic studies of the roles of a suspected factor in the etiology of a disease may be observational or experimental. The essential difference between experimental and observational studies is that in experimental investigations
    a. The study and control groups are equal in size.
    b. The study is prospective.
    c. The study and control groups are always compatible.
    d. The investigator determines who shall be exposed to the suspected factor and who shall not.
    e. Controls are used.

53. Which of the following factors is the most important to the validity of the conclusions drawn from a clinical trial?
    a. equal numbers of treated individuals and those given placebos
    b. follow-up of 100% of the participants
    c. effective randomization of participants
    d. a relatively high incidence of the disease in the population studied
    e. inclusion in both groups of individuals of all ages

54. In a cohort study of a disease, the cohort originally selected consisted of
    a. subjects who are found to have the disease
    b. subjects without the disease
    c. subjects with the factor under investigation
    d. subjects with a family history of the disease
    e. subjects without the factor under investigation

55. Table A3–1 shows the results from a study of the determinants of juvenile delinquency. What would you conclude from these results?
   a. Broken homes seem to be a cause of juvenile delinquency.
   b. Both broken homes and high socioeconomic status independently are causes of juvenile delinquency.
   c. The effect of broken homes should be examined with each socioeconomic class.
   d. Neither of the above statements can be made because the proportions are too small.
   e. Socioeconomic status determines both broken homes and juvenile delinquency.

Table A3–1 Determinants of Juvenile Delinquency

	Percent Delinquency According to Type of Home	P
Children from broken homes	14	<0.05
Children from intact homes	5	

	Percent Delinquency According to Socioeconomic Status of Family	
Children from high SES	16	<0.05
Children from low SES	4	

56. A "double blind" study of a vaccine is one in which
   a. The study group receives the vaccine and the control group receives a placebo.
   b. Neither observer nor subjects know the nature of the placebo.
   c. Neither observer nor subjects know which subject receives the vaccine and which receives a placebo.
   d. Neither the study group nor the control group knows the identity of the observers.
   e. The control group does not know the identity of the study group.

57. A major weakness of case-control studies of the role of a suspected factor in the etiology of a disease, as compared with prospective studies, is that
   a. They are more costly and take longer.
   b. There may be bias in determining the presence or absence of the suspected factor.
   c. There may be bias in determining the presence or absence of the resulting disease.

d. It is more difficult to obtain controls.

e. It is more difficult to assure comparability of cases and controls.

58. A cohort must have
    a. same year of birth
    b. passage through the same time period
    c. common place of residence
    d. exposure to the same disease
    e. common disease history

59. At the initial examination in the Framingham study, coronary heart disease was found in 5 per 1,000 men aged 30 to 44 and in 5 per 1,000 women aged 30 to 44. The inference that in this age group men and women have an equal risk of developing coronary heart disease is
    a. correct
    b. incorrect because of failure to distinguish between incidence and prevalence
    c. incorrect because a proportionate ratio is used when a rate is required to support the inference
    d. incorrect because of failure to recognize a possible cohort phenomenon
    e. incorrect because there is no control or comparison group

60. Which of the following is an advantage of a case-control study?
    a. There is little or no bias in assessment of exposure to the factor.
    b. Multiple disease outcomes following a selected exposure can be readily studied.
    c. Dependence on recall by subjects in the study is minimized.
    d. It is possible to determine the true incidence rate of the disease.
    e. It may be used to study etiology of a rare disease.

61. An orthopedic surgeon published the data relating to the management of 204 patients, who sustained fractures of the femoral neck. Table A3–2 gives mortality data relating to patients who were treated surgically (by open reduction with pinning) or conservatively (by closed reduction with immobilization).

Table A3–2 Mortality Rates for Patients with Surgical Treatments or Conservative Management

	Surgical Treatments	*Conservative Management*	*Total*
Number of Patients	139	65	204
Survivors	103	34	137
Deaths	36	31	67
Percent mortality	26.5%	47.7%	32.9%

$\chi^2 = 8.57$; $P < 0.01$

The most reasonable interpretation of the data is

a. The statistically significant decrease noted in the mortality rate of the patients who underwent surgery means that surgery is the treatment of choice in fractures of the femoral neck.

b. The unusually large number of patients in the surgical group distorts the results.

c. No interpretation is possible because information is lacking on the residual functional disability of patients in both groups.

d. Patients being managed conservatively may be older and sicker than those selected for surgery.

e. The data are useless in that deaths subsequent to discharge are not given.

62. In 1945, there were 1,000 women who worked in a factory painting radium dials on watches. The incidence of bone cancer in these women up to 1975 was compared with that of 1,000 women who worked as telephone operators in 1945. Twenty of the radium dial painters and four of the telephone operators developed bone cancer between 1945 and 1975. This study is an example of a

a. cohort study

b. experimental study

c. clinical trial

d. cross-sectional study

e. case-control study

63. A common medical belief states that after a certain surgical operation it is dangerous for women to have children. An interested physician studied the records of a group of women who had survived this operation. For each woman the records showed the number of children born and the number of years the women lived after the operation. The physician observed that on the average the more children a woman bore after the operation the longer she lived. He concluded the traditional medical belief was a fallacy. This conclusion is incorrect because

a. The doctor's sample was biased since it included only survivors of the operation.

b. The longer a woman lives after the operation, the more children she is likely to have.

c. The doctor should have concluded that the traditional belief is correct.

d. The older women in the group were probably past childbearing age.

e. The older women probably did not survive the operation.

64. The following vaccine trial was performed: 1,000 randomly selected children two years of age were given a vaccine against a certain disease and followed for 10 years. Of these, 80% were never afflicted with the disease. Which is the most correct conclusion regarding the efficacy of the vaccine?

a. The vaccine is an excellent one because of the high rate of immunization.
b. No conclusion is possible since no follow-up was made of nonvaccinated children.
c. The vaccine is not very effective because it should have produced a higher immunization rate.
d. No conclusion is possible since no test of statistical significance was performed.
e. The significant figure is 100% − 80% = 20%, the rate of acquiring the illness.

65. In a study designed to measure the frequency of minor symptoms due to administration of a drug:
   a. Control subjects who receive no medication are necessary in order to interpret the data.
   b. Control subjects who receive a placebo are necessary in order to interpret the data.
   c. The inclusion of control subjects is likely to mislead the investigator, especially if the incidence of adverse reaction is low.
   d. The desirability of having controls depends on the kind of reactions expected.
   e. The desirability of having controls depends on their ages.

66. The data from a study of age versus prevalence of obesity are shown in Table A3–3.

Table A3–3 Age Versus Prevalence of Obesity

Age	Percent Obese
10–40	19
40–60	25
60–80	15
80+	5

The inference that as people grow older they become thinner is
a. correct
b. incorrect because a rate is necessary to support the observation
c. incorrect because no control or comparison group is used
d. incorrect because no such conclusion should be made from cross-sectional data
e. incorrect because prevalence is used whereas incidence is necessary

67. Which of the following is a case-control study?
    a. Study of previous mortality and/or morbidity trends to permit estimates of the occurrence of disease in the future.
    b. Analysis of previous research in different places and under different circumstances to permit establishment of a hypothesis based on cumulative knowledge of all known factors identified in the disease under study.
    c. Obtaining histories and other information from a group of known cases and from a comparison group to determine the relative frequency of characteristics under study in cases.
    d. Study of relative risk of cancer among men who have quit and controls who still smoke.
    e. A survey of the prevalence of a disease in the different strata of a population.

K-Type Questions

Key

a	b	c	d	e
1, 2, 3	1 and 3	2 and 4	only 4	all 4
are correct	are correct	are correct	is correct	are correct

68. "Matching" is undertaken in a case-control study so that
    1. Variables already known to influence the distribution of the disease under study are controlled for in both case and comparison groups.
    2. The influence of the variables matched for may be studied.
    3. The result may not be attributed to the influence of the matched variables.
    4. The study results may include inferences about the influence of the preselected matching variables.
69. To be causally related to a disease, an etiological factor must satisfy the following conditions.
    1. The factor is found more frequently among the diseased than the nondiseased.
    2. Exposure to the factor must precede the development of the disease.
    3. Elimination of the factor reduces the risk of the disease.
    4. The factor is found among all cases of the disease.
70. Controls are needed in a case-control study because
    1. They are matched to the cases for suspected etiological factors.
    2. They may be followed to determine if they develop the disease in question.
    3. They increase the sample size, so that statistical significance may be achieved.

4. They allow evaluation of whether or not the frequency of a characteristic or past exposure among the cases is different from that among comparable people in the population who are free of the disease.

71. In 1975, an investigator performed a computerized search of records in a large obstetrical registry to identify women who were delivered of female babies between 1950 and 1959. From these records he identified women given diethylstilbestrol (DES) during pregnancy and a comparable group not treated with DES or other estrogen-containing formulation. After appropriate permissions were obtained, the daughters, if living, were interviewed and provided with free gynecological examinations to detect any evidence of vaginal neoplasia. Death certificates and medical records were reviewed for all deceased daughters to established the cause of death.

    Which of the following terms may be correctly applied to describe this investigation?
    1. observational
    2. experimental
    3. cohort
    4. case-control

72. In a clinical trial, which of the following are appropriate conditions for exclusion of subjects?
    1. subjects who fail to comply with pre-randomization (before random allocation) screening examinations
    2. subjects who fail to comply with the intervention after having been randomly allocated to study groups
    3. people already receiving the study intervention before subjects have been randomly allocated to study groups
    4. control subjects receiving the study intervention via their private physicians

73. Which of the following are assumptions that underlie standard life table analysis?
    1. Subjects who withdraw or are lost during the course of the study experience the same risk as those who continue.
    2. Withdrawals occur evenly over time within intervals of analysis.
    3. The risk of the study outcome must be constant within each interval.
    4. Subjects who experience the study outcome do not differ in any way from those who do not.

74. Which of the following are assumptions that underlie Kaplan-Meier life table analysis?
    1. Withdrawals occur evenly over time within intervals of analysis.
    2. The risk of the study outcome must be constant within each interval.
    3. Subjects who experience the study outcome do not differ in any way from those who do not.

    4. Subjects who withdraw or are lost during the course of the study experience the same risk as those who continue.

75. Which assumption(s) apply to Cox regression models but not to life tables?
    1. Subjects who withdraw or are lost during the course of the study experience the same risk as those who continue.
    2. The risk of the study event is constant over time for each dependent variable.
    3. Withdrawals occur evenly during intervals of analysis.
    4. The relative risk of the study outcome is constant over time for each dependent variable.

Self-Assessment Final

Objectives Covered: 1–45

Best Choice—Select *One* Answer Only

76. The number of new cancer cases (per 100,000 population) per year for selected sites occurring in men aged 55 to 59 in two populations is shown in Table AF–1.

Table AF–1 Cancer in Men Aged 55 to 59

	Number of New Cases per 100,000 Men per Year	
	Population A	Population B
Lung	40	55
Colon and rectum	20	30
Prostate	12	15

The inference that men aged 55 to 59 in population B are more prone to cancer of the lung, colon and rectum, and prostate than are men aged 55 to 59 in population A is

a. correct

b. incorrect because of failure to distinguish between incidence and prevalence

c. incorrect because proportionate mortality alone does not give an estimate of risk

d. incorrect because of failure to adjust for differences in the age structure of the two populations

e. incorrect because there is no control or comparison group

77. In the investigation of an epidemic of food poisoning at a banquet, high attack rates were found for people who ate roast beef as well as those who ate mushroom sauce. Table AF–2 shows combinations of the two foods that were then considered.

Table AF–2 Attack Rates for Food Combinations

	Ate Mushroom Sauce			Did Not Eat Mushroom Sauce		
	Number	Number Ill	Attack Rate (%)	Number	Number Ill	Attack Rate (%)
Ate roast beef	150	105	70	72	2	3
Did not eat roast beef	42	33	78	26	0	0

Thus, the infective item is most likely to be
a. mushroom sauce
b. roast beef
c. the combination of roast beef with mushroom sauce
d. mushroom sauce without roast beef
e. neither roast beef nor mushroom sauce

78. In an advertisement for raspberry-flavored aureomycin it was claimed that, "Out of 1,000 children with upper respiratory tract infection treated with our raspberry-flavored aureomycin, 970 were asymptomatic within 72 hours." The inference that for a child with upper respiratory tract infection, raspberry-flavored aureomycin is the treatment of choice is
a. correct
b. incorrect because the comparison is not based on rates
c. incorrect because no control or comparison group is used
d. incorrect because no test of statistical significance is made
e. incorrect because a cohort effect may be operating

79. A study covering records of 300 deaths in white children from accidental poisoning reported in city A showed that among those who died, there were five times as many children whose socioeconomic conditions were rated as low than there were children whose socioeconomic conditions were rated as high. The inference that accidental poisoning is five times more common among children from families of low socioeconomic status than among those of high socioeconomic status in city A is
a. correct
b. incorrect because the study and comparison groups are not comparable or relevant
c. incorrect because there is improper interpretation of statistical significance
d. incorrect because the comparison is not based on rates
e. incorrect because observer or interviewer bias may account for the results

80. Community A and community B each have crude mortality rates for coronary heart disease (CHD) of 4 per 1,000. The age-adjusted CHD mortality rate is 5

per 1,000 for community A and 3 per 1,000 for community B. One may conclude that

   a. Community A has a younger population than community B.

   b. Community A has an older population than community B.

   c. The two communities have identical age distribution.

   d. Diagnosis is more accurate in community A than in community B.

   e. Diagnosis is less accurate in community A than in community B.

81. A case-control study is characterized by all except the following:

   a. It is relatively inexpensive.

   b. Relative risk may be estimated from the results.

   c. Incidence rates may be computed.

   d. One selects controls without the disease.

   e. Assessment of past exposure may be biased.

82. The risk of acquiring a disease is measured by the

   a. incidence rate

   b. incidence rate times the average duration of the disease

   c. incidence rate divided by the prevalence rate

   d. prevalence rate

   e. prevalence rate times the average duration of the disease

83. A study of traffic safety in Minnesota showed that 61% of those involved in accidents last year had more than 10 years of driving experience, 21% had 6 to 10 years of experience, and 17% had 1 to 5 years of experience. Traffic experts concluded that experience seems to make drivers more complacent and careless. Which of the following best states why this conclusion is not justified?

   a. The rates have not been standardized for age differences.

   b. The data are incomplete because of unreported accidents.

   c. A comparison needs to be made with similar data on drivers not involved in accidents.

   d. No test of statistical significance has been made.

   e. Prevalence is used where incidence is required.

84. The strength of an association between a factor and a disease is best measured by

   a. incubation period

   b. incidence of the disease in the total population

   c. prevalence of the factor

   d. attributable risk

   e. relative risk

85. Table AF–3 shows the relative frequency of newly reported cancers of specific sites in two populations.

Table AF–3 Relative Frequency of Cancers in Two Populations

	Percent of Total	
Site of Cancer	Population A	Population B
Lung	10.0	6.7
Breast	30.0	20.0
Uterus	25.0	16.7
All other	35.0	56.6
Total: all sites	100.0	100.0

The inference that population A seems to be more prone to cancer of the lung, breast, and uterus than is population B is

a. correct

b. incorrect because of failure to distinguish between incidence and prevalence

c. incorrect because a proportionate ratio is used when a rate is required to support the inference

d. incorrect because of failure to recognize a possible cohort phenomenon

e. incorrect because there is no control or comparison group

86. An investigation of an outbreak of diarrhea revealed that the proportion of cases eating in restaurant A was 85%, in restaurant B was 15%, and in restaurant C was 55%, and the proportion consuming public water was 95%. Which of the following statements is correct?

a. The source is restaurant A because it has the highest proportion of cases among the restaurants.

b. The source is not restaurant B because it has the lowest rate.

c. The source is the water supply because it has the highest proportion of cases.

d. The source could be either restaurant A, restaurant C, or the water supply.

e. Similar data on a well group must be collected to reach a valid conclusion.

87. *Case fatality rate* for a given disease refers to

a. the crude mortality rate per 100,000 population

b. cause-specific mortality rate due to the disease

c. a fatal outcome of any disease

d. the percentage of deaths among cases of the disease

e. the proportion of deaths due to the disease among all deaths from all causes

88. An investigator is interested in the etiology of neonatal jaundice. To study this condition, he selected 100 children who were diagnosed with this condition and 100 children born in the same time period and in the same hospital who did not have a diagnosis of neonatal jaundice. He then reviewed the obstetrical and delivery records of their mothers to determine various prenatal and perinatal exposures. This is an example of a
    a. cross-sectional study
    b. case-control study
    c. cohort study
    d. clinical trial
    e. an experiment
89. A study of all women aged 20 to 25 years old in a large industrial state found that the annual rate of new cases of cervical cancer in women who used oral contraceptives was 5/100,000 and that it was 2/100,000 in those who did not use oral contraceptives. On the basis of these data, the inference that taking oral contraceptives causes cervical cancer is
    a. correct
    b. incorrect due to failure to distinguish between incidence and prevalence
    c. incorrect due to failure to adjust for possible differences in age distributions of users and nonusers
    d. incorrect because a proportion is used when a rate is required to support the inference
    e. incorrect because the two groups may differ in other relevant factors
90. Which of the following statements describes the major advantages of a randomized clinical trial?
    a. It avoids observer bias.
    b. It lends itself to ethical justification.
    c. It yields results replicable in other patients.
    d. It rules out self-selection of participants to the different treatment groups.
    e. It enrolls representative patients.
91. A survey conducted in England revealed that of 224 families in which there had been a known case of poliomyelitis, 56 maintained parakeets as a family pet. In another British survey, 30 of 99 poliomyelitis patients questioned kept parakeets. The inference that there is some relationship between the presence of a parakeet in a household and the occurrence of poliomyelitis among household members is
    a. correct
    b. incorrect because of failure to distinguish between incidence and prevalence
    c. incorrect because a proportionate ratio is used when a rate is required to support the inference

d. incorrect because of failure to recognize a possible cohort phenomenon

e. incorrect because there is no control or comparison group

92. A controversy occurred between the proponents of drug therapy and remedial reading for patients with dyslexia. To support their position, one party wrote, "Of 119 patients with dyslexia, 97 showed improvement following remedial reading courses." The inference that in patients with dyslexia, remedial reading is the therapy of choice is

    a. correct

    b. incorrect because the comparison is not based on rates

    c. incorrect because no control or comparison group is being used

    d. incorrect because no test of statistical significance is being made

    e. incorrect because a cohort effect may be operating

93. An investigator determines the correlation coefficient between triglyceride levels and degree of atherosclerosis in sampled blood vessels to be + 1.67. On the basis of this you would conclude that

    a. Triglyceride level is a good predictor of atherosclerosis.

    b. Triglyceride level is not a good predictor of atherosclerosis.

    c. High triglyceride levels cause atherosclerosis.

    d. Atherosclerosis causes high triglyceride levels.

    e. The investigator has incorrectly determined the correlation coefficient.

Table AF–4 describes the survival of cancer patients following a new drug treatment.

Table AF–4 Survival of Cancer Patients Following Drug Treatment

Interval	Patient Alive at Beginning of Interval	Patients Who Died during Interval	Proportion of Those Alive at Beginning of Interval Who Died during Interval
0–3 months	1,000	300	0.3
3–6 months	700	140	0.2
6–12 months	560	112	0.2
12–18 months	448	224	0.5
18–24 months	224	90	0.4

Use these data for questions 94 through 96.

94. The probability that a patient survives for two years after the treatment, given that he has survived for six months, is

    a. 134/560 = 0.24

    b. 426/560 = 0.76

c. 134/700 = 0.19

d. 426/700 = 0.61

e. cannot be determined from these data

95. The probability that a patient survives for three months after the treatment began is

a. 0.3

b. 0.4

c. 0.5

d. 0.6

e. 0.7

96. The probability that a patient dies within two years after the treatment is

a. 90/224 = 0.4

b. 866/1000 = 0.866

c. 90/1000 = 0.09

d. 224/1000 = 0.224

e. cannot be determined from these data

97. A study was conducted to assess a new surgical procedure designed to reduce the incidence of postoperative complications. The incidence of complications was found to be 40% in 25 patients having the new procedure and 60% for 20 patients having the old procedure. This difference is not statistically significant. Thus, it may be concluded that

a. The new procedure is effective in reducing postoperative complications.

b. The new procedure is ineffective in reducing postoperative complications.

c. The sample is biased.

d. The result is clinically significant.

e. The evidence is insufficient to demonstrate that the new procedure is effective in reducing postoperative complications.

98. A screening test of known sensitivity and specificity is applied to two populations. The prevalence of the disease being screened for is 10% in population A and 1% in population B. Which of the following is true?

a. The percent of all negative tests that have false-negative results is lower in population A than in population B.

b. Specificity is lower in population A than in population B.

c. Reliability is higher in population A than in population B.

d. The percent of all positive tests that have false-positive results is lower in population A than in population B.

e. Sensitivity is higher in population A than in population B.

99. Two plans for the follow-up treatment of newly detected hypertensives were tried in a community. Plan A was used in the eastern and southern districts of the community while Plan B was used in the northern and western districts. Table AF–5 shows the data obtained three years after the start of these plans.

Table AF–5 Success Rates of Two Plans in Treating Hypertensives

	Plan A	Plan B
Number of hypertensives	2,200	1,900
Percent of hypertensives successfully treated	41	45

The differences in success rates for the two plans were statistically significant ($P < 0.01$). Health officials, however, decided not to change to plan B in the eastern and southern districts because the magnitude of the difference was so small. This implies that

a. They attributed the difference in success rates to chance alone.
b. They feel the samples were too small to justify a decision in favor of plan B.
c. They felt the P value was too small to justify a decision in favor of plan B.
d. They distinguished between statistical significance and practical importance of the difference in success rates.
e. They felt that the success rates should be higher than 50%.

100. Serum cholesterol levels are obtained for four healthy men. The probability that all will fall below the 10th percentile of the distribution of cholesterol for healthy males is
    a. 0.4
    b. $1 - (0.1)^4$
    c. $(0.1)^4$
    d. $(0.9)^4$
    e. cannot be determined from these data

101. In a diabetes detection program, the screening level for a positive blood sugar level in test 1 is set at 160 mg/dl and in test 2 at 130 mg/dl. The sensitivity is
    a. greater in test 1
    b. greater in test 2
    c. equal in tests 1 and 2
    d. dependent on the size of the population being evaluated
    e. dependent on the actual prevalence of diabetes in the population

102. One thousand patients who were seen at the emergency department of a large urban hospital for possible myocardial infarction (MI) had serum drawn for laboratory evaluation. Of the total, 300 were later found not to have had an MI. The triglyceride results in this group were compared with those of the MI group, and Table AF–6 was generated.

Table AF–6 Association Between Triglyceride Level and Myocardial Infarction

Group	MI	Non-MI
High triglyceride	600	100
Normal triglyceride	100	200

These results persisted even after controlling for age, race, sex, and cholesterol level differences, and the conclusion was drawn that subjects with high triglyceride levels were at greater risk of an MI is
a. justified
b. not justified because the data were not based on a community sample
c. not justified because there is no proper control group
d. not justified because the same association would be seen if MI led to increased triglyceride levels
e. not justified because the subjects were not matched on the confounders

Matching

Match each of the following analytical models to one, and only one, of the study objectives listed below:

a. simple least squares regression
b. multiple least squares regression
c. logistic regression
d. Cox proportional hazards regression
e. none of the above

_____103. To describe the distribution of cholesterol in a middle-class black community.
_____104. To predict the survival time for breast cancer patients from tumor characteristics measured at the time of diagnosis.
_____105. To obtain the relative risk of developing heart disease during a 10-year time period associated with smoking 10 or more cigarettes daily while controlling for other risk factors.
_____106. To describe the expected weight of infants in their first year according to their age in months.
_____107. To predict serum triglyceride levels of middle-aged men from seven dietary factors.

K-Type Questions

Key

a	b	c	d	e
1, 2, 3	1 and 3	2 and 4	only 4	all 4
are correct	are correct	are correct	is correct	are correct

108. A report of a clinical trial of a new drug versus a placebo noted that the new drug gave a higher proportion of success than did the placebo. The report ended with the statement $\chi^2 = 4.72$, $P < 0.05$. In light of this information, we may conclude
    1. Fewer than 1 in 20 will fail to benefit from the drug.
    2. The chance that an individual patient will fail to benefit is less than 0.05.
    3. If the drug were effective, the probability of the reported finding is less than 1 in 20.
    4. If the drug were ineffective, the probability of the reported finding is less than 0.05.

109. In a study designed to determine the five-year incidence of hypertension in an inner-city community, a 15% random sample of normotensives is selected for follow-up. Which of the following should be done to avoid a biased estimate of incidence of hypertension in the community?
    1. Repeated attempts should be made to contact members of the sample who are difficult to reach for follow-up measurements.
    2. Death certificates should be examined for members of the sample who died in the five-year period to determine if their deaths were hypertension related.
    3. Efforts should be made to locate members of the sample who move out of the community during the five-year period so that their blood pressure status can be determined.
    4. Members of the sample who refused to have their blood pressure taken during the follow-up should be replaced by residents who are more cooperative.

110. A study of mortality patterns in 41 states found a correlation coefficient of +0.64 between cigarettes sold per capita and death rates for cancer of the esophagus. The P value is less than 0.001. Which of the following are compatible with this finding?
    1. Cigarette smoking is a cause of cancer of the esophagus.
    2. States with high cigarette consumption rates have populations that are more susceptible to cancer of the esophagus for reasons other than smoking.

    3. States with high cigarette consumption rates have environmental features that increase the risk of cancer of the esophagus.

    4. Chance alone accounts for the association between cigarette consumption and esophageal cancer.

111. The IQs of a class of students are distributed according to the normal curve, with a mean of 115 and a standard deviation of 10. This means that

    1. 50% will have IQs less than 115.

    2. 5% will have IQs less than 105.

    3. 2.5% will have IQs greater than 135.

    4. 2.5% will have IQs greater than 125.

112. To determine attack rates for a respiratory disease of unknown origin among people attending an American Legion Convention in Philadelphia, random samples of guests staying at four hotels were surveyed for subsequent illness. Since it was not feasible to survey all the guests, random sampling provided the best information because

    1. It would identify all cases of the disease.

    2. It would avoid biases introduced by the method of selecting guests for study.

    3. It would eliminate sampling error.

    4. It would give each guest an equal chance of being selected.

113. A series of 1,000 female patients with breast cancer contained 32 who were pregnant. From this, one may conclude

    1. Pregnancy is a rare complication of breast cancer.

    2. If age adjustments are made we can determine the risk of breast cancer during pregnancy.

    3. Breast cancer is a rare complication of pregnancy.

    4. In this series 3.2% of the breast cancer patients were pregnant.

114. In a study to determine whether or not tonsillectomy is associated with subsequent development of Hodgkin's disease, the estimated relative risk of developing the disease for those with a prior tonsillectomy was found to be 2.9. From this we may conclude

    1. The case fatality rate is higher among those with a prior tonsillectomy.

    2. The rate of Hodgkin's disease cases is higher among those with a prior tonsillectomy.

    3. Tonsillectomy appears to protect against the development of Hodgkin's disease.

    4. The incidence of Hodgkin's disease among those with a prior tonsillectomy is 2.9 times that of those with intact tonsils.

115. Correct statements concerning case control and cohort studies include

    1. Cohort studies are likely to be less susceptible to bias.

    2. Cohort studies permit direct determination of incidence rates.

3. The case-control approach has the advantage that data are readily at hand for quick analysis.
4. The cohort approach is often used to elucidate factors related to rare disease.
116. Table AF–7 shows the incidence of retrolental fibroplasia (RLF) by sex of the infant at the Boston Lying-In Hospital, 1938–1952.

Table AF–7 Incidence of Retrolental Fibroplasia

		RLF	
	Number of Premature Infants	Cases	Percent
Males	260	45	17.3
Females	321	54	16.8

The chi-square value was found to be 0.02 and the P value was greater than 0.10. The implication of this result is that
1. The sex of the infant is probably not a determinant of RLF.
2. It is probable that the difference in incidence of RLF between the sexes can be explained by chance alone.
3. The difference in incidence of RLF between the sexes is not statistically significant.
4. RLF is probably associated with sex of the infant.
117. In general, screening should be undertaken for diseases with the following features:
1. diseases for which there is an effective primary prevention measure available
2. diseases with a high prevalence in distinct segments of the population
3. diseases that are readily diagnosed and for which no treatment is available
4. diseases with a natural history that can be altered by medical intervention
118. Table AF–8 shows the data from a comparison of mortality rates due to cancer of the uterus in users and nonusers of supplemental estrogen.

Table AF–8 Mortality Rates from Uterine Cancer

	Mortality Rates (per 100,000)	
	Age 40–54	Age 55–70
Users of estrogen	3.0	17.0
Nonusers	1.0	6.0

Valid conclusions derived from the above data concerning mortality among estrogen users include

1. The mortality rates for cancer of the uterus are higher in estrogen users in both age groups studied.
2. A causal relationship is demonstrated between the use of estrogen and incidence of uterine cancer.
3. Mortality from cancer of the uterus rises with age regardless of whether or not estrogen is used.
4. The mortality rate is lower in nonusers than users because the symptoms of uterine cancer are detected earlier in the former group of women.

119. Data for patients at a certain hospital show the mean length of stay is 10 days and the median is 8 days. The most frequent length of stay is 6 days. From these facts we conclude

1. Approximately 50% of the patients stay less than 6 days.
2. The distribution of length of stay is not symmetrical.
3. The standard deviation is 2 days.
4. The mean length of stay is affected by stays of very long duration.

120. A random sample of teenage prenatal patients seen at University Hospital during 1973 had a mean hematocrit of 29 with a standard error of 1.5. From this information we may conclude that

1. The normal range for hematocrit among teenage prenatal patients is 26 to 32.
2. It is to be expected that 95% of all teenage prenatal patients will have hematocrit levels between 26 and 32.
3. The range 26 to 32 will include 95% of all teenage prenatal patients seen at University Hospital in 1973.
4. The range 26 to 32 will include the mean of all teenage prenatal patients seen at University Hospital in 1973 with 95% probability.

121. The median survival time of children with leukemia treated with a combination of drugs and radiation is reported to be 28.2 months. This implies that

1. A child with leukemia treated with a combination of drugs and radiation can be expected to survive 56.4 months.
2. Half of the children with leukemia treated with a combination of drugs and radiation survive more than 28.2 months.
3. None of the children with leukemia treated with a combination of drugs and radiation survive beyond 56.4 months.
4. Half of the children with leukemia treated with a combination of drugs and radiation survive less than 28.2 months.

122. Which of the following are correct inferences that may be drawn from Table 15–3 (see p. 146)?

1. The probability of surviving to the third month after surgery is about 70% in both cohorts 1 and 2.

2. The probability of surviving from the 3rd month to the beginning of the 13th month is equal in both groups.
3. Given that a patient has survived to the 3rd month, his probability of surviving to the 13th month in the low T5 group is 74% and in the high T5 group is 58%.
4. The greatest difference in survival between groups occurs at the start of the 49th month.

123. Censoring in a prospective study whose end point is mortality occurs when
   1. The study ends before all subjects have died.
   2. Subjects die before the planned termination of the study.
   3. Subjects withdraw (alive) from the study.
   4. Subjects are excluded from study because of the presence of a particular factor or complication.

The relative risks found in Table AF–9 were formed as the ratio of unadjusted inpatient mortality rates associated with two medical procedures in hospital A relative to hospital B. Use these data to answer question 124.

Table AF–9 Relative Risks of Two Medical Procedures (Between Two Hospitals)

Procedure	Relative Risk (A/B)	P Value
Cesarean section	0.5	0.05
Coronary artery bypass	2.0	0.10

124. Which of the following are valid interpretations of these data?
   1. The risk of mortality associated with coronary bypass surgery is approximately twice as great in hospital A as in hospital B, but this difference is not statistically significant.
   2. The risk of death from Cesarean section differs little between hospitals, but the small difference is statistically significant.
   3. The relative risk of death from Cesarean section is twice as great in hospital B as in hospital A, and this difference is statistically significant.
   4. The P values suggest that the risk of death from Cesarean section is nearly twice as important as that arising from coronary artery disease.

125. Which of the following are true of a double-blind placebo-controlled randomized clinical trial?
   1. Both the intervention and control groups consist wholly of blind patients.
   2. Neither the investigator nor the patient is aware of who is receiving the intervention and who is not.
   3. The trial involves only sugar pills.
   4. The control group receives an "inert vehicle" that mimics all the facets of the intervention except the specific "active" component being evaluated.

Answers to Self-Assessments

1. b	26. a	51. b	76. a	101. b
2. b	27. b	52. d	77. a	102. d
3. b	28. c	53. c	78. c	103. e
4. e	29. e	54. b	79. d	104. d
5. c	30. c	55. c	80. a	105. c
6. c	31. b	56. c	81. c	106. a
7. c	32. c	57. b	82. a	107. b
8. c	33. a	58. b	83. c	108. d
9. c	34. b	59. b	84. e	109. a
10. b	35. d	60. e	85. c	110. a
11. a	36. c	61. d	86. e	111. b
12. e	37. c	62. a	87. d	112. c
13. e	38. c	63. b	88. b	113. d
14. e	39. a	64. b	89. e	114. c
15. c	40. d	65. b	90. d	115. a
16. b	41. c	66. d	91. e	116. a
17. d	42. b	67. c	92. c	117. c
18. a	43. d	68. b	93. e	118. b
19. b	44. e	69. a	94. a	119. c
20. d	45. c	70. d	95. e	120. d
21. a	46. d	71. b	96. b	121. c
22. b	47. a	72. b	97. e	122. b
23. c	48. c	73. a	98. d	123. b
24. b	49. b	74. d	99. d	124. b
25. e	50. c	75. d	100. e	125. c

Glossary

Included below are terms that are recurrent themes in epidemiology and biostatistics. Not included are terms that are the foci of specific chapters and are defined when they are introduced. For a more complete reference the reader is directed to: *A Dictionary of Epidemiology* by John M. Last published in 1983 by Oxford University Press, New York.

GENERAL TERMS

Association—Variables are related if knowledge of one is useful in predicting the other (e.g., exposure is related to disease if knowledge of exposure status is useful in predicting disease risk or vice versa).

Bias—Systemic error.

Confounding factor—A variable that is related to both the exposure and the disease under study and that serves as a bridge to mediate an apparent association between the exposure and disease where no real association exists; or, alternatively, it may mask a real association.

Effect modifier—A variable that changes the association between two other variables, e.g., exposure to asbestos increases the risk of lung cancer among smokers but not nonsmokers, thus smoking serves to modify the effect of asbestos on lung cancer risk.

Epidemic—A marked increase in the occurrence of disease over and above expectation for a defined community during a defined time period.

Variable—A factor of interest that assumes different values such as age, gender, and disease status.

RATE TERMINOLOGY

Adjusted rate—An expression of the predicted number of health events within a standard population defined by one or more variables not under study and used to control for effects mediated by such variables (e.g., the age-adjusted death rate is 6.2 deaths per 1,000 persons).

Crude rate—An expression of the observed number of health events per unit of the population at risk in a defined time period (e.g., crude mortality rate of 5.7 deaths per 1,000 persons in 1985).

Specific rate—An expression of the observed number of health events within a defined subgroup or stratum of the population at risk within a defined time period (e.g., age-specific death rate of 1.2 deaths per 1,000 persons aged 10 to 19).

STATISTICAL TERMS

Confidence interval—The range that will include, with a stated probability, the actual population parameter estimated from a sample (e.g., based on a random sample, it can be stated with 95% certainty that the mean fasting blood sugar of the population of a given zip code lies between 95 and 105 mg/dl).

***P* value**—The probability of obtaining a given result by chance alone.

Probability—The likelihood of an event usually expressed as the proportion of those experiencing the event of those who *could* experience the event (those at risk).

Random sample—A subgroup drawn from a population such that each member has a known chance of inclusion, thus permitting inferences about the population to be derived from analysis of the sample.

Statistical significance—Implies that the observed result was unlikely to have occurred by chance alone; usually based on a *P* value less than 0.05.

STUDY DESIGN TERMS

Blinding—In a study, either the subject, or the observer, or preferably both (double-blinded) are kept unaware (blinded) of the treatment group to which the subject is assigned so that the responses or recorded observations cannot be influenced by preconceived notions of the efficacy of the intervention.

Control group—The group of subjects who lack the attribute under investigation but are otherwise as similar as possible to the study group (e.g., the unexposed in a cohort study or those free of disease in a case-control study).

Hypothesis—Educated guess about an association that is testable in a scientific investigation.

Matching—The process of selecting study and control group subjects so that they are similar with respect to confounding factors.

Study group—The group of subjects who have the attribute under investigation in a research project (e.g., the disease in a case-control study, the exposure in a cohort study).

Target population—That population about which study inferences, usually based on a sample, are to apply.

RISK TERMINOLOGY

Absolute risk—A statement of the magnitude of disease in a sample or a population, usually estimated by disease incidence.

Relative risk—A statement of the relative magnitude of the risk of disease in one group compared with another, usually derived from a comparison of incidence rates (e.g., persons who smoke have five times the annual incidence of lung cancer compared with nonsmokers; for smokers the relative risk of lung cancer is 5).

Risk factor—A characteristic that is of value in predicting risk (e.g., people with high cholesterol have an increased risk of heart disease; therefore, cholesterol is a risk factor for heart disease).

Index

Note: Page numbers in *italics* denote figures and exhibits; those followed by "t" denote tables.